P9-AGP-986

WETLAND ECONOMICS, 1989–1993

WETLAND ECONOMICS, 1989–1993

A Selected, Annotated Bibliography

Compiled by
Jay A. Leitch
and
Herbert R. Ludwig, Jr.

Bibliographies and Indexes in Economics and Economic History, Number 17

GREENWOOD PRESS
Westport, Connecticut • London

Library of Congress Cataloging-in-Publication Data

Leitch, Jay A.
    Wetland economics, 1989–1993 : a selected, annotated bibliography
/ compiled by Jay A. Leitch and Herbert R. Ludwig, Jr.
       p.   cm.—(Bibliographies and indexes in economics and
economic history, ISSN 0749–1786 ; no. 17)
    Includes indexes.
    ISBN 0–313–29286–8 (alk. paper)
    1. Wetland conservation—Economic aspects—Bibliography.
2. Wetlands—Economic aspects—Bibliography. I. Ludwig, Herbert R.
II. Title. III. Series.
Z7405.W47L45   1995
[QH75]
016.33391′ 8—dc20   94–39564

British Library Cataloguing in Publication Data is available.

Library of Congress Catalog Card Number: 94–39564
ISBN: 0–313–29286–8
ISSN: 0749–1786

First published in 1995

Greenwood Press, 88 Post Road West, Westport, CT 06881
An imprint of Greenwood Publishing Group, Inc.

Printed in the United States of America

∞™

The paper used in this book complies with the
Permanent Paper Standard issued by the National
Information Standards Organization (Z39.48–1984).

10 9 8 7 6 5 4 3 2

CONTENTS

ACKNOWLEDGMENTS

We could not have completed this work without the support, encouragement, and assistance of numerous persons and agencies. The Department of Agricultural Economics, the Water Resources Research Institute, and the North Dakota Agricultural Experiment Station at North Dakota State University all provided support for this effort and receive our sincere appreciation.

In accessing the works included in this book, the Interlibrary Loan staff at the North Dakota State University Library made an invaluable contribution in securing hundreds of documents. Without their help and the cooperation of other libraries, we could not have produced such an extensive and complete book.

Our appreciation is extended to JoAnn Thompson, who served as our word processing specialist, and to Brett Hovde, Becky Leitch, and Lisa Roberts, who helped identify, locate and abstract documents.

Finally, we thank the many authors and organizations who identified and provided copies of relevant documents.

OVERVIEW

Wetlands have been a major source of land use policy controversy in the United States and worldwide for at least a decade. The published literature across many disciplines has grown and continues to grow rapidly. The issues are extremely complex in terms of science, politics, economics, and social values. The economics, assessment, and valuation literature addresses the focal point of trade-offs and choice making relative to a scarce resource. Persons involved in every aspect of the wetland debate can make use of economic valuation information.

The purpose of this bibliography is to bring together the salient works on the economic and related restoration and delineation aspects of wetland resources.

WETLAND PRIMER

Background in a variety of areas, beginning with a sense of wetlands as part of the natural landscape, is helpful to fully appreciate the range of wetland issues. An excellent introduction to wetlands and source of natural science information about wetlands is *The Audubon Society Nature Guide to Wetlands* (Niering 1988). The *Guide*'s introduction provides an overview of wetlands and wetland functions. The remainder of the *Guide* is devoted to the flora and fauna of North American wetlands. Countless other printed sources of natural history aspects of wetlands exist and are available in most public libraries.

For an academic and rigorous treatment of wetland and wetland issues, Mitsch and Gosselink's (1993) textbook, *Wetlands*, is as comprehensive as a single volume can be. The second edition includes a chapter on history, three chapters on definitions and wetland types, four chapters on physical and natural sciences aspects of wetlands, seven chapters addressing characteristics of general wetland ecosystems, and finally, four chapters on management.

Wetland identification and delineation are not well sorted out at this point, which remains one of the barriers to consensus about wetland management. The current guide for federal agencies is the *1987 Corps of Engineers Wetlands Delineation Manual* (Environmental Laboratory 1987). Other useful references include *Classification of Wetlands and Deepwater Habitats of the United States* (Cowardin et al. 1979) and *Wetlands of the United States*, also known as *Circular 39* (U.S. Department of the Interior 1956).

An historical introduction to regulation and protection of wetlands can be found in either *Wetlands: Their Use and Regulation* (U.S. Office of Technology Assessment 1984) or *Our National Wetland Heritage: A Protection Guidebook* (Kusler 1983). More recently, the Council for Agricultural Science and Technology's (1994) *Wetland Policy Issues* monograph discusses wetland policy in general.

Only three scientific journals specifically address wetland issues. They are *Wetlands*, journal of the Society of Wetland Scientists; *Wetland Journal*; and *Wetlands Ecology and Management*. The *National Wetlands Newsletter* is a good source for current wetland policy information.

SCOPE

The focus of this book is wetland economic assessment and valuation as it pertains to policy making and other wetland policy-related issues. Biological or ecological assessment and valuation literature are not included, unless they have an economics component.

Most of the literature pertains to the United States and Canada, although relevant international works are also included. The time frame is roughly 1989 to 1993, but earlier relevant works not identified in Leitch and Ekstrom (1989) are included, as well as some early 1994 publications. Professional journals, books, university research reports, conference proceedings, government documents, industry reports, and selected unpublished papers and popular media accounts are included. Most of the literature included should be readily attainable through libraries accessible to the general public.

Criteria for inclusion of works include methodological, empirical, or policy contribution; timeliness; and availability.

PROCEDURE

Since publication of the first wetland economics bibliography (Leitch and Ekstrom 1989), the principal author has routinely collected literature in anticipation of an updated bibliography. A thorough search of appropriate indexes and professional journals was made in addition to searches of computer databases. Eight electronic databases were searched. The most readily available source of information was on the PALS network, which allowed electronic searching of numerous libraries. The *AGRICOLA* database was searched to find agricultural related citations. *Current Contents* was searched in agriculture, biology and environmental science, and social and behavioral sciences. Finally, a *Dialog* Search was conducted for material published since 1988 in (1) dissertation abstracts, (2) Enviroline, (3) CAB abstracts, (4) water resources abstracts, and (5) WATERNET. These computerized databases were searched using the keywords

> wetland, pothole, fen, estuary, bog, marsh, swamp, bayou, coast, and riparian

cross-referenced with

> economic, use, utilize, value, valuation, drain, conserve, mitigation, creation, construction, delineation, identification, assess, develop, optimal, human, method, conversion, investment, price, pay, benefit, cost, manage, GIS, character, recreation, loss, function, profit, or restoration.

Finally, notice was sent to selected scientists and professional association newsletters asking for help identifying the literature, especially that which may not have reached the usual bibliographic sources.

ORGANIZATION

Each of the four general subject area sections of the bibliography is preceded by a short overview of the literature. The subject area sections are

> *Wetland Economics, Methodological*
> *Wetland Economics, Empirical*
> *Wetland Restoration/Creation Economics*
> *Wetland Delineation/Definition Issues*

Entries are organized alphabetically by author within each section. Entries are cross-listed where they may fall into more than one subject area.

Entries are indexed three ways, using citation numbers and not page numbers as references. The Author Index includes all authors and/or editors. The Geographic Index lists entries pertaining to specific geographical locales. Finally, the Subject Index was developed to help readers locate entries addressing similar subject areas.

REFERENCES

Council for Agricultural Science and Technology. 1994. *Wetland Policy Issues.* Comments from CAST No. CC1994-1, Ames, Iowa.

Cowardin, L.M., V. Carter, F.C. Golet, and E.T. LaRoe. 1979. *Classification of Wetlands and Deepwater Habitats of the United States.* FWS/OBS-79/31, Fish and Wildlife Service, U.S. Department of the Interior, Washington, D.C.

Environmental Laboratory. 1987. *1987 Corps of Engineers Wetland Delineation Manual.* Technical Report Y-87-1, Waterways Experiment Station, U.S. Army Corps of Engineers, Vicksburg, Mississippi.

Kusler, Jon A. 1983. *Our National Wetland Heritage: A Protection Guidebook.* Environmental Law Institute, Washington, D.C.

Leitch, Jay A. and Brenda L. Ekstrom. 1989. *Wetland Economics · and Assessment: An Annotated Bibliography.* Garland Publishing, Inc., New York.

Mitsch, William J. and James G. Gosselink. 1993. *Wetlands.* Second Edition, Van Nostrand Reinhold, New York.

Niering, William A. 1988. *The Audubon Society Nature Guide to Wetlands.* Third printing, Alfred A. Knopf, New York.

U.S. Department of the Interior. 1956. *Wetlands of the United States.* Circular 39, Fish and Wildlife Service, Washington, D.C.

U.S. Office of Technology Assessment. 1984. *Wetlands: Their Use and Regulation.* Congress of the United States, U.S. Government Printing Office, Washington, D.C.

WETLAND ECONOMICS, 1989–1993

WETLAND ECONOMICS, METHODOLOGICAL

OVERVIEW

Three advances have been made in the theory of wetland economics over the past five years. First, there has been a small increase in the body of basic economics. Second, there has been a modest increase in the number of empirical analyses of wetland values. Finally, economic theory found its way into far more corners of the wetland issue than previously. In short, we know what we knew better and we use it more.

The small increase in the body of basic economic science applicable to wetland economics has generally come about through modest enhancements in the methods for assigning dollar values to extra-market goods and services such as Contingent Valuation Methods (CVM). These contributions are generally found in the professional journals of applied economics such as the *Journal of Environmental Economics and Management, Ecological Economics,* and *Land Economics* and are only included here if they have been applied specifically to value wetlands.

While the state of the art in practical evaluation methods may have moved forward slightly, most of the contributions have been more academic than practical. This is so because existing methods of economic analyses are generally adequate for wetland evaluation, and have little need of being "fine-tuned" until companion, compatible improvements are made in several other wetland-related disciplines. Because applied economists are near the top of the information food chain, they are dependent upon sufficient and relevant information emanating from the physical and natural sciences.

As practitioners, not necessarily trained in economics, have tried to pull together the web of information necessary to evaluate wetlands, some meaningful incorporation of environmental-ecological principles and concepts into economic evaluations has begun to take place, and vice versa. This increment has been reported in a growing body of literature. This literature mainly attempts to explain, integrate, or apply existing tools of environmental and resource economics to wetland situations.

In the past five years, a few new names (e.g., Bardecki 1989; King 1992) have appeared in the wetland economics theory literature. Yet the earlier works of Shabman and Batie (1989); Leitch and Shabman (1988); Thomas, Liu, and Randall (1982); Goldstein (1971); and others remain as foundations of wetland valuation theory. Recent contributions have led to increased understanding of the issues from an economic perspective and to a heightened awareness of the need to carry out interdisciplinary research in wetland valuation studies.

REFERENCES

Bardecki, Michal J. 1989. "The Economics of Wetland Drainage." *Water Quality Bulletin* 14:76-80, 103-104.

Goldstein, Jon H. 1971. *Competition for Wetlands in the Midwest: An Economic Analysis.* Resources for the Future, Inc., Johns Hopkins Press, Baltimore, Maryland.

King, Dennis M. 1992. "The Economics of Ecological Restoration." Chapter 19 in *Natural Resource Damage Assessment: Law and Economics,* John Duffield and Kevin Ward, eds., John Wiley Publishers, New York.

Leitch, Jay A. and Leonard A. Shabman. 1988. "Overview of Economic Assessment Methods Relevant to Wetland Evaluation." Pp. 95-102 in *The Ecology and Management of Wetlands: Volume 2--Management, Use, and Value of Wetlands,* D. D. Hook, W. H. McKee, Jr., H. K. Smith, J. Gregory, V. G. Burrell, Jr., M. R. DeVoe, R. E. Sojka, S. Gilbert, R. Banks, L. H. Stolzy, C. Brooks, T. D. Matthews, and T. H. Shear, eds., Timber Press, Portland, Oregon.

Shabman, L. A. and S. S. Batie. 1990. "Estimating the Economic Value of Coastal Wetlands: Conceptual Issues and Research Needs." Pp. 3-15 in *Estuarine Perspectives,* Victor S. Kennedy, ed., Academic Press, New York.

Thomas, Margaret, Ben-chieh Liu, and Alan Randall. 1979. *Economic Aspects of Wildlife Habitat and Wetlands.* Midwest Research Institute, Kansas City, Missouri.

SELECTED BIBLIOGRAPHY

1. Adamus, P. R. 1991. "Data Sources and Evaluation Methods for Addressing Wetland Issues." Appendix to a report of the World Wildlife Fund, Washington, D.C.

2. Adamus, Paul R. 1992. *A Process for Regional Assessment of Wetland Risk.* Environmental Research Laboratory, U.S. Environmental Protection Agency, Corvallis, Oregon, 17 pp. plus 156 pp. in appendices.
Illustrates one means of "Best Professional Judgement" in the context of risk assessment using a process that incorporates available literature and information from a panel of regional experts. Uses the Prairie Pothole Region (PPR) of the U.S. as an example for assessing and prioritizing the risks to valued functions (e.g., wildlife production) as a result of wetland loss (through both conversion and degradation). The fundamental question being addressed is "Which valued, difficult to replace, PPR wetland functions are subject to the greatest losses, and from what?" The report is printed in four separately bound volumes: (1) summary report; (2) Appendix A: Results of Application of the Risk Assessment Process; (3) Appendix B: Technical Documentation, Prairie Pothole Region; and (4) Appendix C: Conceptual Process Model for Basin-Type Wetlands of the Prairie Pothole Region.

3. Allen, Geoffrey P. and Thomas H. Stevens. 1983. *Use of Hedonic Price Technique to Evaluate Wetlands.* No. 136, Water Resources Research Center, University of Massachusetts, Amherst, 42 pp.
Concludes that the property value technique of estimating the economic value of wetlands and open space between residential areas and shorelines for nine areas in Massachusetts may be inappropriate for valuation of non-unique wetland resources.

4. Anderson, Robert and Mark Rockel. 1991. *Economic Valuation of Wetlands.* American Petroleum Institute, Washington, D.C., 60 pp.
Explores the role of economics in guiding wetland policy and use decisions. Asserts that all but a handful of the studies estimating the economic value of wetlands are severely flawed as most of the studies examine only a subset of wetland functions. Contends that mitigation and mitigation banking requirements often delay unreasonably the issuance of permits.

5. Aylward, B. and E. B. Barbier. 1992. "Valuing Environmental Functions in Developing Countries." *Biodiversity and Conservation* 1(1):34-50.
    Presents methods of evaluating environmental functions in developing countries. Uses tropical forests, wetlands, and biodiversity as examples. Reviews existing studies and makes recommendations for future research.

6. Barbier, Edward B. 1993. "Valuing Tropical Wetland Benefits: Economic Methodologies and Applications." *The Geographical Journal* 159(1):22-32.
    States that, too often, development decisions are made without considering the loss in wetland benefits arising from damages and conversion. Often the underlying assumption is that the benefits to society of any development option must presumably be greater than any loss. Applications suggest the basic method for assessing and valuing the economic benefits of tropical wetlands is relatively straightforward, but difficult to apply because of data and resource constraints. The analysis shows that wetlands can yield substantial economic returns to local inhabitants, and these benefits should not be excluded as an opportunity cost of any scheme which reduces wetland systems.

7. Barbier, Edward B. 1994. "Valuing Environmental Functions: Tropical Wetlands." *Land Economics* 70(2):155-173.
    Discusses the valuation of environmental functions of tropical wetlands, focussing, in particular, on the regulatory ecological functions in support of protection of economic activities. The problem associated with valuation is illustrated through the use of a basic model indicating the costs and benefits of converting or diverting wetland resources to alternative uses. The model indicates that failure to consider foregone net benefits of *in situ* use of wetland resources can lead to an under estimation of alternative uses of these resources and their excessive appropriation from wetlands. Approaches the problem of valuation from a production function approach. Uses an example of a single use of wetland resources and also discusses the further problems associated with multiple use. Concludes by offering some additional steps required to develop analytical techniques and applications which may have wider relevance in developing countries.

8. Bardecki, Michal J. 1987. *Wetland Evaluation: Methodology Development and Pilot Area Selection.* Report 1 of *Wetlands are not Wastelands,* Sustainable Development Branch, Canadian Wildlife Service and Wildlife Habitat Canada, Ottawa, 114 pp.
    First in a seven-part series. Describes three evaluation techniques: (1) willingness-to-pay, (2) opportunity cost, and (3) multi-objective evaluation

(trade-off approach). Selects four wetland sites as case study sites for these techniques: (1) Greenock Swamp in Ontario; (2) Cowichan Estuary Wetlands on Vancouver Island, British Columbia; (3) Miscou Island Bog in New Brunswick; and (4) Redvers Area Potholes in Saskatchewan. Results of the pilot study for each area are in entries 94, 138, 233, and 274.

9. Bardecki, Michal J. 1989. *Synthesis of Pilot Study Results.* Report 6 of *Wetlands are not Wastelands,* Sustainable Development Branch, Canadian Wildlife Service and Wildlife Habitat Canada, Ottawa, 27 pp.
Summarizes the willingness-to-pay, opportunity cost, and cumulative assessment approaches to wetland evaluation according to strengths, weaknesses, and applicability of the methods, data, and expertise needed for their implementation. See entries 9, 20, 94, 138, 233, 274 for results of individual pilot studies and 8 for a description of the three evaluation techniques.

10. Bardecki, M. J. 1989. "The Economics of Wetland Drainage." *Water Quality Bulletin* 14:76-80, 103-104.
Explains the differences between social and private benefits regarding wetland drainage and conservation.

11. Bardecki, Michal J., Wayne K. Bond, and E. W. Manning. 1988. "Wetland Evaluation and the Decision-Making Process." Pp. 525-534 in *Proceedings of the VIIth International Water Resources Association World Congress on Water Resources: Water for Development,* International Water Resources Association, Urbana, Illinois.
Identifies the limitation of traditional techniques of weighting wetland values as opposed to others potentially derived from other uses of these areas. Presents three methods for reflecting societal benefits of wetlands: willingness-to-pay, opportunity cost, and cumulative impact approach (based on appraisal of the loss of wetland function).

12. Bardecki, Michal J., Wayne K. Bond, and E. W. Manning. 1989. "Assessing Greenock Swamp: Functions, Benefits, and Values." Pp. 235-244 in *Wetlands: Inertia or Momentum,* Michal J. Bardecki and Nancy Patterson, eds., Federation of Ontario Naturalists, Don Mills, Ontario, Canada.
Assesses three alternative evaluation methods: (1) willingness-to-pay approach, (2) opportunity cost approach, and (3) cumulative assessment approach. Applies these methods to Greenock Swamp, Ontario. Explains

that the approaches cannot be comprehensive because (1) there is general imperfection in the understanding of wetland functions, (2) there are data problems, (3) values cannot be derived as generally, (4) opportunity costs are limited because certain values are not fully reproducible, and (5) average values of wetland functions possibly may not provide for a method to derive marginal values. Included in entry 14.

13. **Bardecki, Michal J., E. W. Manning, and Wayne Bond. 1989. "Practical Methods for Valuing Wetlands: An Assessment of Three Approaches." Pp. 367-371 in** *Wetlands and River Corridor Management: Proceedings of an International Symposium,* **Jon A. Kusler and Sally Daly, eds., Association of Wetland Managers, Inc., Omnipress, Madison, Wisconsin.**
Describes three approaches to the valuation of wetlands: (1) an approach based on willingness-to-pay for wetland values and functions, (2) an opportunity cost approach to be applied to measurable wetland values and to the proposed alternate use, and (3) a cumulative assessment approach synthesizing a broader range of social goals and objectives than those generally encompassed by the term *economic.* Case studies are also provided. Included in entry 177.

14. **Bardecki, Michal J. and Nancy Patterson, eds. 1989.** *Wetlands: Inertia or Momentum.* **Federation of Ontario Naturalists, Don Mills, Ontario, Canada, 426 pp.**
Proceedings of a conference held in Toronto, Ontario on October 21-22, 1988. Themes include hydrology and chemistry, biology, inventory, stewardship, management issues, and economic evaluation. Includes entries 12, 35, 42, 65, 95, and 252.

15. **Bennett, J. and I. Goulter. 1989. "The Use of Multiobjective Analysis for Comparing and Evaluating Environmental and Economic Goals in Wetland Management."** *GeoJournal* **18(2):213-220.**
Examines how multiobjective methods can be applied to the evaluation and comparison of economic and, more particularly, environmental objectives for wetland projects. Objectives and conflicts generally present in wetlands management are also discussed, such as between the use of fertilizers in agriculture and its effects on aquaculture.

16. **Bergstrom, John C., John Stoll, John P. Titre, and Vernon L. Wright. 1989. "Economic Value of Wetland-Based Recreation."** *Ecological Economics* **10:111-118.**
An empirical study was conducted to measure expenditures and consumers' surplus associated with on-site, current recreational uses of a

coastal wetlands area. Aggregate expenditures were estimated at approximately $118 million and aggregate consumers' surplus was estimated at approximately $27 million per year. These results suggest that the economic impacts and net economic benefits associated with wetlands-based recreation may be substantial. Hence, recreational functions provided by wetlands may be important considerations for wetlands policy and management.

17. **Bergstrom, John C. and John R. Stoll. 1989. "Recreational Benefits of Wetland Protection."** Pp. 38-46 in *Alternative Perspectives on Wetland Evaluation and Use*, E. Jane Luzar and Steven A. Henning, eds., SNREC Publication No. 27, Southern Rural Development Center, Mississippi State University, Mississippi State.
Presents a model for assessing the economic value of wetlands. Discusses the empirical estimation of wetlands-based recreation in Louisiana based on the concept of "willingness-to-pay" derived from the results of a two-wave mail survey of Louisiana. Included in entry 192.

18. **Bergstrom, J. C. and J. R. Stoll. 1993. "Value Estimator Models for Wetlands-Based Recreational Use Values."** *Land Economics* 69(2):132-137.
Evaluation and implementation of policies affecting wetlands management may require measurement of the economic value of the policies to individuals and groups. A potentially powerful means for measuring changes in wetlands-based recreational values is the use of value estimator models. The general specification and potential applications of value estimator models for wetlands-based recreational use values are discussed in this paper. Future research needs are also identified.

19. **Bergstrom, C. J., R. Stoll, and A. Randall. 1990. "The Impact of Information on Environmental Commodity Valuation Decisions."** *American Journal of Agricultural Economics* 72(3):614-621.
Develops a conceptual model which provides insight into how information affects willingness-to-pay for environmental commodities. Found that information is important for accurate consumer valuations of environmental commodities.

20. **Bond, Wayne K., Michal J. Bardecki, Kenneth W. Cox, and Edward W. Manning. 1988.** *Interim Report.* **Report 2 of** *Wetlands are not Wastelands*, **Sustainable Development Branch, Canadian**

Wildlife Service and Wildlife Habitat Canada, Ottawa, 16 pp.
Reviews methods and study site selections discussed in *Wetland Evaluation: Methodology Development and Pilot Area Selection*, Report 1 (see entry 8), and gives first results for the study areas.

21. **Bowers, J. 1988. "Cost-benefit Analysis in Theory and Practice: Agricultural Land Drainage Projects." Pp. 265-289 in *Sustainable Environmental Economics and Management: Principles and Practice*, R. Kerry Turner, ed., Belhaven Press, London.**
Studies the practice of cost-benefit analysis in the United Kingdom land drainage industry. The study is based on an examination of cost-benefit analyses of drainage schemes from, or for, statutory drainage bodies. Concludes that the institutional structure within which land drainage proposals are formulated and appraised is a central issue in the problem of land drainage. Argues that the requirement that analysts and decision-makers should not have prior commitment to the outcome of CBA is not satisfied. As a result, pressures exist to interpret the rules and to modify them in ways which are favorable to land drainage. Recommends that a property rights approach to public sector investment decision making would place it in the center of the stage. Included in entry 73.

22. **Cable, Ted T., Virgil Brack, and Virgil R. Holmes. 1989. "Simplified Method for Wetland Habitat Assessment." *Environmental Managment* 13(2):207-213.**
Presents a wetland Habitat Assessment Technique (HAT) using birds as indicators of habitat quality. HAT can provide input to more extensive evaluation techniques. Measures of species diversity and rarity are used to assess the quality of the wetland. By applying the notion of ecologically optimum size, the technique addresses the issue of economic efficiency. Results of field testing HAT on 11 tidally influenced wetlands are presented to illustrate HAT's utility.

23. **CAST. 1994. *Wetland Policy Issues*. Council for Agricultural Science and Technology, Ames, Iowa, 47 pp.**
Explains and summarizes wetland policy issues, including wetland definition and delineation; functions and values of wetlands; agricultural conflicts with wetlands; socioeconomic issues; and wetland conservation concepts. Concludes there is scarce middle ground in discussions of wetlands, wetland values in the absolute are of little value without relative values of other landscapes and land uses, the public is largely oblivious to the wetlands debate, wetlands are social concepts and not ecological concretes, and that science has made contributions toward resolving the issues but it is more than just a scientific issue.

24. **Coker, Annabel and Cathy Richards, eds. 1992.** *Valuing the Environment: Economic Approaches to Environmental Evaluation.* **Belhaven Press, London, 184 pp.**
The volume is the result of a workshop of ecologists and economists devised to better the methods for assessing coastal management problems. Includes nine chapters, each with a central theme, and a corresponding commentary for each chapter. The book explores issues such as valuing environmental goods, cost/benefit analysis, economic issues raised by valuing environmental goods, survey based valuation methods, and some procedural guidelines.

25. **Costanza, R., Stephen C. Farber, and Judith Maxwell. 1989.** **"Valuation and Management of Wetland Ecosystems."** *Ecological Economics* **1(4):335-361.**
Employed both willingness-to-pay and energy-based methodologies to determine a range of wetland values in Louisiana. Estimates of the total present value of an average acre of natural wetlands in Louisiana were $2,429-$6,400 per acre (assuming an 8 percent discount rate) to $8,977-$17,000 per acre (assuming a 3 percent discount rate). The paper discusses the fundamental theoretical and practical problems underlying natural resource valuation, summarizes methods and findings for Louisiana wetlands, and elaborates on some of the more recalcitrant problems attending applied natural resource valuation. Includes discussion of the discounting problem as applied to natural resources and argues for lower discount rates for valuing renewable natural resources than apply for other aspects of the economy.

26. **Costanza, Robert and Lisa Wainger. 1991. "Ecological Economics."** *Business Economics* **26(4):45-48.**
Recommends that environmental elements be incorporated into economic assessments; indicators can be modified by ecological factors to produce an index of sustainable economic welfare. Public policy can include incentives for resolving environmental problems.

27. **Cox, Kenneth W., Michal Bardecki, Wayne Bond, and Ted Manning. 1990. "Wetlands are Not Wastelands: Better Procedures and Methods for Indicating the True Value of Renewable Resources to Society."** Pp. 196-201 in *Wetlands of the Great Lakes: Protection and Restoration Policies--Status of the Science,* **Jon A. Kusler and Richard Smardon, eds., Proceedings of an International Symposium, Association of State Wetland Managers, Inc., Berne, New York.**
Reviews progress in the "Wetlands are not Wastelands" project and suggests future initiatives. See entry 8. Included in entry 178.

28. **Dalecki, M. G., J. C. Whitehead, and G. C. Bloomquist. 1993.
"Sample Non-Response Bias and Aggregate Benefits in Contingent Valuation: An Examination of Early, Late, and Non-Respondents."** *Journal of Environment Management* **38:133-143.**
Uses the example of a western Kentucky wetland for testing non-response bias in a contingent valuation mail survey. Found that there was no difference between respondents and nonrespondents if the early and late responses are similar. Concludes that the range of aggregate benefit narrows as response rates increase and nonresponse bias decreases.

29. **de Groot, Rudolf S. 1992.** *Functions of Nature: Evaluation of Nature in Environmental Planning, Management and Decision Making.* **Wottery-Noordhof, The Netherlands, 315 pp.**
A textbook, written by an ecologist, with a major emphasis on socio-economic evaluation of environmental functions. Brings together ecological and economic concepts in a comprehensive method whereby all functions and values of ecosystems can be assessed and evaluated in a systematic manner. Uses tropical moist forests and a tidal wetland (the Dutch Wadden Sea) as two of three case studies. Discusses conceptual issues and provides tentative monetary assessments of the socio-economic functions of these two wetland resources.

30. **Dixon, John A. and Paul B. Sherman. 1990.** *Economics of Protected Areas: A New Look at Benefits and Costs.* **Island Press, Washington, D.C., 234 pp.**
Part one of the book demonstrates how economics can be used to improve the decision-making process involving natural areas such as comparing benefits and costs, valuation techniques, and selection of protected areas. The approach is aimed at resource managers, planners, and analysts in national governments and aid agencies who must make decisions on land use and the allocation of funds for protected areas. Economics are incorporated into the decision-making process to take into account all the benefits and costs of the alternative being considered. Part two examines the application of this approach in various locations around the world, including a wetland area in Thailand.

31. **Douglas, Aaron J. 1989.** *Annotated Bibliography of Economic Literature on Wetlands.* **Research and Development, Fish and Wildlife Service, U.S. Department of the Interior, Washington, D.C., 67 pp.**
Contains 90 annotated references focusing on valuation problems that arise from wetlands allocation issues and conflicts. Concentrates on the seminal works of the field.

32. **Feitelson, Eran. 1992. "An Alternative Role of Economic Instruments: Sustainable Finance for Environmental Management."** *Environmental Management* **16(3):299-307.**
Discusses the use of economic instruments, such as effluent fees and tradeable discharge permits, as a cost effective and efficient means for reducing pollution. Examines the use of economic instruments for estuary protection. Shows that economic instruments have the potential of serving as sustainable funding sources for a wide variety of actions and jurisdictions involved in estuarine control and management programs.

33. **Fisk, David W., ed. 1990.** *Wetlands: Concerns and Successes-- Proceedings of a Symposium.* **American Water Resources Association, Bethesda, Maryland, 586 pp.**
Includes chapters on wetlands inventory and assessment, wetlands and stormwater management programs, wetland preservation, mitigation and creation, wetland values and function, wetlands management, and planning and policy. Includes entries 96, 127, 152, 155, 290, 439, and 457.

34. **Gan, Christopher E. and E. Jane Luzar. 1993. "Conjoint Analysis of Wetland-Based Recreation Activities."** **Pp. 330-335 in** *Wetlands: Proceedings of the 13th Annual Conference, Society of Wetland Scientists, New Orleans, Louisiana,* **Mary C. Landin, ed., South Central Chapter, Society of Wetland Scientists, Utica, Mississippi.**
Focuses on the application of conjoint analysis in the estimation of wetland-based recreation experiences in Louisiana. Waterfowl hunters' site preferences were evaluated, comparing private (leased) versus public sites. Results indicate that two management issues, length of the hunting season, and daily bag limit, and one site related factor, the rate of congestion, were significant factors influencing waterfowl hunters' trip rating preferences. Included in entry 49.

35. **Gibson, Robert B. and Graham Whitelaw. 1989. "Environmental Assessment and Agricultural Drainage."** **Pp. 279-288 in** *Wetlands: Inertia or Momentum,* **Michal J. Bardecki and Nancy Patterson, eds., Federation of Ontario Naturalists, Don Mills, Ontario, Canada.**
Discusses the potential of Ontario's environmental assessment process to provide a mechanism for management of the remaining wetlands in southern Ontario. Concludes that a somewhat unconventional approach using the existing provision of the Environmental Assessment Act could provide for more creative development and evaluation of a "drainage

management plan" involving a package of planning, regulatory, and economic initiatives. Included in entry 14.

36.   Gray, Elaine. 1991. *Wetlands: A Partially Annotated Bibliography.* Council of Planning Librarians, Chicago, Illinois, 19 pp.

37.   Hanemann, M., J. Loomis, and B. Kanninen. 1991. "Statistical Efficiency of Double-bounded Dichotomous Choice Contingent Valuation." *American Journal of Agricultural Economics* 73(4):1255-1263.
       Found that the "double-bounded" approach is shown to be asymptotically more efficient than the conventional "single-bounded" approach. Using data from a survey of Californians regarding their willingness-to-pay for wetlands in the San Joaquin Valley, it is shown that, in a finite sample, the gain in efficiency can be very substantial.

38.   Hawkins, Darroll Lee. 1993. *The Passive Benefits of Urban Wetlands: A Model for Assessing Monetary Worth (Wetlands).* Ph.D. thesis, University of Louisville, Louisville, Kentucky, 145 pp., (University Microfilms Inc., Order No: AAD93-32932).
       Dollar values for urban wetlands are assessed using replacement cost of functions.

39.   Henderson, James E. 1993. "Limited by Science or Economics?: Use of Economic Analysis in the Corps of Engineers Permitting Activities." Pp. 336-341 in *Wetlands: Proceedings of the 13th Annual Conference, Society of Wetland Scientists, New Orleans, Louisiana,* Mary C. Landin, ed., South Central Chapter, Society of Wetland Scientists, Utica, Mississippi.
       Discusses the difficulties of applying economic principles to wetland issues as economic analysis is constrained by limits of scientific analysis of wetland functions, and the determination of public demand and values. Concludes that the Corps' research effort will develop guidance for incorporating economic and public use values into the public interest review process. Included in entry 49.

40.   Hickman, C. A. 1990. "Forested Wetland Trends in the United States: An Economic Perspective." *Forest Ecology and Management* 33-34(1-4):227-238.
       Describes the evolution of wetland economics with an economic explanation of past wetland losses, and the role of externalities. Explains the role of economics for future studies.

41. **Hook, Donal D. and Russ Lea, eds. 1989.** *Proceedings: Symposium on The Forested Wetlands of the Southern United States.* **Southeastern Forest Experiment Station, Forest Service, U.S. Department of Agriculture, Asheville, North Carolina, 168 pp.**
Presents 25 papers in five categories: (1) nonpoint sources of pollution and the functions and values of wetlands; (2) best management practices for forested wetlands; (3) streamside management strategies; (4) sensitive areas management; and (5) balancing best management practices and water quality standards for feasibility, economic, and functional effectiveness. Includes entry 271.

42. **Jorjani, Hamid and Peter Duinker. 1989. "An Approach for Evaluating Trade-Offs Between Agricultural Drainage and Wetland Conservation."** Pp. 261-277 in *Wetlands: Inertia or Momentum,* **Michal J. Bardecki and Nancy Patterson, eds., Federation of Ontario Naturalists, Don Mills, Ontario, Canada.**
Develops a set of system indicators as part of a comprehensive framework for evaluating the expected performance of agricultural drainage programs. These indicators involve several hydrological, biochemical, ecological, and finance factors both at the farm and societal levels. Proposes methods whereby the monetary equivalent of each indicator may be estimated. Discusses its current implementation as a case study in Ontario, Canada. Included in entry 14.

43. **Kiker, Clyde F. and Gary Lynne. 1989. "Can Mama Help? Multiple Alternative/Multiple Attribute Evaluation of Wetlands."** Pp. 25-37 in *Alternative Perspectives on Wetland Evaluation and Use,* **E. Jane Luzar and Steven A. Henning, eds., SNREC Publication No. 27, Southern Rural Development Center, Mississippi State University, Mississippi State.**
Evaluates the multiple alternative/multiple use evaluation approach as a method for assessing the important decisions associated with wetland permits. The paper is presented in five sections. The first section gives a brief overview of wetland processes and human activities that affect them. A framework for envisioning potential conflicts among uses is offered. The second section briefly discusses the regulatory context and the breadth of factors to be considered is noted. The difficulty associated with economic valuation of wetlands is discussed in the third section. The fourth section presents the "multiple alternative/multiple attribute evaluation" information presentation approach. Plus a concluding section. Included in entry 192.

44. **King, Dennis M. and Curtis C. Bohlen. 1994. "Compensation Ratios for Wetland Mitigation: Guidelines and Tables for Applying the**

Methodology." In *Wetland Mitigation: A Framework for Determining Compensation Ratios,* a report prepared for the Office of Policy Analysis, U.S. Environmental Protection Agency, Washington, D.C.

45. **Kiviat, Erik. 1991.** *Wetland Human Ecology (Cultural Adaption).* **Ph.D. thesis, The Union Institute, Cincinnati, Ohio, 187 pp., (University Microfilms Inc., Order No: AAD92-11445).**
Nineteen non-industrialized wetland-based or associated cultures worldwide are examined for their dependence upon wetland functions. Cross-tabulates 19 environmental attributes of wetlands and 157 culture traits to develop an Environmental Harshness Index. Concludes that wetland alteration by small-scale societies is not unlike alteration by complex societies.

46. **Kraft, Steven E., Paul Dye, Andrew French, Richard Johnson, Roger Beck, and Dennis Robinson. 1991. "Preservation and Restoration of Wetlands: The Challenge of Economic-Ecological Input/ Output Modeling."** *American Journal of Agricultural Economics* **73(5):1523.**
Discusses the problems associated with conducting economic impact analyses for wetland areas located in sparse economic regions. Problems addressed covered the meshing of ecological and economic concerns within the framework of traditional input-output analysis, problems with existing data bases and their frequently incompatible scales of reference, use of the biosphere reserve model for combining economic and ecological data to enhance ecological diversity while maintaining the greatest number of options for using the buffer areas, evaluation of ecological functions, and the use of hybrid input-output models.

47. **Kusler, Jon A. and Gail Brooks, eds. 1987.** *Proceedings of the National Wetland Symposium: Wetland Hydrology.* **Technical Report 6, Association of Wetland Managers, Inc., Berne, New York, 339 pp.**
Collection of papers designed to help wetland managers (regulators, planners, researchers, waterfowl managers) understand wetland hydrology, its relationship to various wetland functions, the impact of various activities on hydrology, and approaches for reducing or compensating for these projects.

48. **Kusler, Jon A., Sally Daly, and Gail Brooks, eds. 1988.** *Proceedings of the National Wetland Symposium: Urban Wetlands.* **Association of Wetland Managers, Inc., Berne, New York, 402 pp.**

Contains 65 papers centered around the central theme of urban wetlands. Includes many papers that discuss the values of wetlands (descriptive only), wetland delineation, wetland restoration and creation, and wetland regulations. Includes entries 59, 64, 135, 207, 370, 378, 383, 452, and 461.

49. **Landin, Mary C., ed. 1993. *Wetlands: Proceedings of the 13th Annual Conference, Society of Wetland Scientists, New Orleans, Louisiana.* South Central Chapter, Society of Wetland Scientists, Utica, Mississippi, 990 pp.**
Contains 191 papers and 38 posters which cover a wide array of wetland topics and wetland types covering wetland geology, restoration, and creation, geomorphology, engineering, education, activities on military installations, monitoring, ownership, regulation, ecology, hydrology, evaluation and delineation, stewardship and management, and economics. Includes entries 34, 39, 356, and 422.

50. **Lant, Christopher and Jo Beth Mullens. 1991. "Lake and River Quality for Recreation and Contingent Valuation." *Water Resources Bulletin* 27(3):453-460.**
Offers a broader concept of "lake/river quality" to describe the characteristics that recreationists value in lakes and rivers. This definition is comprised of a collection of physical, ecological, and aesthetic characteristics that create the opportunity for recreation, scenic enjoyment, and fish and wildlife propagation. Claims that the broader concept better meets contingent valuation requirements and should be the basis for defining environmental improvements and declines to be hypothetically sold in contingent valuation surveys.

51. **Lant, C. L. and G. A. Tobin. 1989. "The Economic Value of Riparian Corridors in Cornbelt Floodplains: A Research Framework." *Professional Geographer* 41(3):337-349.**
Claims that market mechanisms can fail to account for many positive attributes of riparian wetland ecosystems. Individual farmers frequently make socially inappropriate decisions regarding floodplain land-uses because the benefits accruing from wetlands, such as improved water quality and enhanced recreational activities, are public goods. A spatial economic model based on willingness-to-pay procedures, assesses the mix of agricultural/wetland uses that compares the marginal value of natural wetland vegetation to agricultural production on rural cornbelt floodplains. In case studies of two river basins, the value of wetland per acre ($102.61 and $1,129.73) was found to be greater than agricultural value ($94.42) for both basins.

52. **Lugo, Ariel E., Mark Brinson, and Sandra Brown, eds. 1990.**
    Ecosystems of the World 15: Forested Wetlands. **Elsevier Science
    Publishing Co., Inc., New York, 527 pp.**
    Intended as an introduction to the subject of forested wetlands. Part one
    reviews the available information on the structure and function of forested
    wetlands, emphasizes concepts, and is strongly biased toward forested
    wetlands in the Caribbean and the U.S. The second part presents case
    studies and descriptions of forested wetlands. The final chapter is a
    synthesis and an effort to present new paradigms of wetland ecology. In-
    cludes items 168 and 396.

53. **Lupi, Frank, Jr., Theodore Graham-Tomasi, and Steven J. Taff.
    1991.** *A Hedonic Approach to Urban Wetland Valuation.*
    **Institute of Agriculture, Forestry and Home Economics,
    University of Minnesota, St. Paul, 29 pp.**
    Examines the extent to which the relationship between property values
    and wetlands can be used to measure the economic value of the non-
    market benefits of wetlands. Some positive relationship between wetlands
    and nearby property values is established. However, available wetland
    data do not all distinguish (1) the exact effects of individual wetlands, (2)
    the effects of small unprotected wetlands not in the data set, and (3) the
    precise effects of being close to wetlands as opposed to being in the
    neighborhood of wetlands. Although the existence of some positive
    relationship between wetland acreage per section was established,
    precisely which values were captured is not clear (i.e., open space, view,
    habitat).

54. **Mackenzie, John. 1993. "A Comparison of Contingent Preference
    Models."** *American Journal of Agricultural Economics* **75(3):593-
    603.**
    Compares the informational efficiencies of contingent rating, contingent
    ranking, and two contingent paired comparison methods as alternatives to
    the referendum contingent valuation method. The contingent rating
    method is hypothesized to be the most efficient because ratings convey
    information on preference intensities and can uniquely represent
    respondent indifference or ambivalence. Survey data on hunters' ratings
    of alternative hypothetical hunting trips are used to estimate four
    alternative indirect utility models from which marginal willingness-to-pay
    measures for individual trip attributes are derived. Model comparison,
    WTP estimates, and their confidence intervals confirm the relative
    efficiency of the contingent rating approach.

55. **Manuel, Patricia Marie. 1992.** *A Landscape Approach to the
    Interpretation, Evaluation, and Management of Wetlands.* **Ph.D.**

thesis, Dalhousie University, Halifax, Nova Scotia, Canada, 523 pp., (University Microfilms Inc., Order No: AADNN-80100).
The regional implications of no-net-loss are discussed with respect to functional values. A five-part method involving the overall wetland-landscape relationship is developed. The difference between this and other approaches is the landscape orientation. Some swamps in Nova Scotia are used as a case study to illustrate somewhat different conclusions from implementing traditional valuation methodologies.

56. **Mitsch, William J. 1991. "Ecological Engineering: Approaches to Sustainability and Biodiversity in the U.S. and China." Pp. 428-448 in** *Ecological Economics: The Science and Management of Sustainability,* **R. Costanza, ed., Columbia University Press, New York.**
Examples of ecological engineering from U.S. and China's culture are presented and overall approaches are compared. Each culture has ecological principles guiding it but approaches environmental pollution built on different economic and social structures. The two approaches may possibly be managed into one ecological engineering paradigm for long-term sustainability of environmental quality. Four ecological engineering case studies from each culture are analyzed. The case studies utilize methods for a variety of uses including wastewater treatment, coal mine drainage, iron retention, food/fuel production, and fodder.

57. **Mitsch, William J. and James G. Gosselink. 1993.** *Wetlands.* **2nd edition, Van Nostrand Reinhold, Florence, Kentucky, 641 pp.**
Contains one chapter on values and valuation of wetlands. Valuation techniques include nonmonetized scaling and weighting approaches for comparing different wetlands or different management options for the same wetland, and common denominator approaches that reduce the various values to some common term such as dollars or embodied energy. Other chapters contain information on wetland environments and ecosystems.

58. **Palmer, James F. 1989. "The Determination of Scenic Quality from River Attributes." Pp. 172-177 in** *Wetlands and River Corridor Management: Proceedings of an International Symposium,* **Jon A. Kusler and Sally Daly, eds., Association of Wetland Managers, Inc., Omnipress, Madison, Wisconsin.**
Reports a reanalysis of scenic river inventory data pursuant to a generic analysis process to demonstrate its usefulness in predicting scenic quality. The method demonstrated assigns weights to river attributes for use in a scenic value index as called for in the Wild and Scenic Rivers Act. Included in entry 177.

59. Palmer, James F. and Richard C. Smardon. 1988. "Visual Amenity Value of Wetlands: An Assessment in Juneau, Alaska." Pp. 104-107 in *Proceedings of the National Wetland Symposium: Urban Wetlands*, Jon A. Kusler, Sally Daly, and Gail Brooks, eds., Association of Wetland Managers, Inc., Berne, New York. Discusses ranking of visual characteristics and their importance in wetland valuation. Included in entry 48.

60. Pearce, David W. and R. Kerry Turner. 1990. *Economics of Natural Resources and the Environment.* The John Hopkins University Press, Baltimore, Maryland, 373 pp. Includes a chapter entitled "A Case Study of Wetlands" as an example of social inefficiency in natural resource use. Describes the total economic value of wetlands, market and intervention failure as a source of inefficiency, methodology to measure wetland use inefficiency, and the mechanisms for social cost intervaluation.

61. Richardson, Curtis J. 1994. "Ecological Functions and Human Values in Wetlands: A Framework for Assessing Forestry Impacts." *Wetlands* 14(1):1-9. Develops an assessment procedure comparing changes in wetland function from both a disturbed and a reference wetland. This approach scales the wetland functions in a reference system to 100 percent and then compares the altered wetland's functional response. Methods to analyze wetland functions in the field are outlined along with examples of the effects of forestry activities on wetland response.

62. Scodari, Paul F. 1990. *Wetlands Protection: The Role of Economics.* Environmental Law Institute, Washington, D.C., 89 pp. Discusses how economic analysis can be used to strengthen wetlands protection efforts. Presents an overview of the complex problem of economic valuation of a living ecosystem. Recommends a need for improved communication between wetland scientists and economists. Outlines recommendations that will increase the accuracy of wetlands valuation in the context of water resources development. Suggests to other researchers the numerous avenues that remain to be explored in future work.

63. Shabman, Leonard. 1991. "Integrating Reconversion of Wetlands into Achieving Environmental Goals in Urbanizing Regions." Pp. 23-28 in *A National Policy of "No Net Loss" of Wetlands: What do Agricultural Economists Have to Contribute?* Ralph E. Heimlich, ed., Staff Report No. AGES 9149, Resources and

Technology Division, Economic Research Service, U.S. Department of Agriculture, Washington, D.C.
Argues the imperative to incorporate basic economic principles in order to achieve the policy goal of no-net-loss of wetlands. Bases arguments on four premises: (1) public concern is for ecosystem functions, not wetlands; (2) some wetlands are not wetlands of regulatory concern; (3) development of wetlands will occur; and (4) wetlands restoration is possible. Included in entry 153.

64. Smardon, Richard C. 1988. "Aesthetics, Recreational, Landscape Values of Urban Wetlands." Pp. 92-96 in *Proceedings of the National Wetland Symposium: Urban Wetlands*, Jon A. Kusler, Sally Daly, and Gail Brooks, eds., Association of Wetland Managers, Inc., Berne, New York.
Describes the extent to which urban wetlands provide socio-cultural benefits and functions. Does not quantify the benefits or functions. Included in entry 48.

65. Smardon, Richard C. 1989. "Developing Socio-Cultural Assessment of Wetland Values in the United States." Pp. 245-253 in *Wetlands: Inertia or Momentum*, Michal J. Bardecki and Nancy Patterson, eds., Federation of Ontario Naturalists, Don Mills, Ontario, Canada.
Outlines current efforts to develop methods and techniques of assessing human use values of wetlands (e.g., recreation, aesthetics, subsistence uses) that can be incorporated within the U.S. Army Corps of Engineers' Wetland Evaluation Technique (WET). Included in entry 14.

66. Stavins, Robert N. 1990. "Alternative Renewable Resource Strategies: A Simulation of Optimal Use." *Journal of Environmental Economics and Management* 19(2):143-159.
Presents a dynamic analysis of resource exploitation in the presence of environmental consequences. Finds that socially optimum use relates to the private market model of wetland exploitation, providing a basis for internalizing environmental externalities thereby creating optimum resource exploitation strategies. Empirical analysis focuses on the Lower Mississippi Alluvial Plain. Concludes that if all of the wetlands in the study area had annual ecological (external) values in the range of $80 to $150 per acre, zero net depletion of forest wetlands in the study area would have occurred during the period 1935-1984. But, actual values of wetlands vary from one area to another--from less than $25/acre annually to as much as $10,000/acre per year. Recommends that, in general, a central goal of new policy should be to eliminate unwarranted public subsidies and internalize environmental externalities.

67. Stavins, Robert N. 1990. *The Welfare Economics of Alternative Renewable Resource Strategies: Forested Wetlands and Agricultural Production.* Garland, New York, 233 pp.
Examines the causes of rapid depletion of forested wetland resources in the U.S. during the past 50 years and contrasts that with socioeconomic perspective. Bridges a model based on rational individual behavior (rather than a representative firm) with statistical models of market performance while maintaining the premise that natural resource exploitation has negative environmental consequences.

68. Taff, Steven J. 1992. *What is a Wetland Worth? Concepts and Issues in Economic Valuation.* Staff Paper P92-1, Department of Agricultural and Applied Economics, University of Minnesota, St. Paul, 23 pp.
A wetland has no economic value in and of itself. Nor does it have a unique value, irrespective of context. Economic value is ascribed to a wetland by humans operating at a confluence of individual preferences, property rights, technological opportunities, and available resources. Such values are not generally reflected in market prices, a deficiency that can nonetheless be addressed by competent economic analysts, using a variety of empirical techniques. The task is complicated by scientific information shortfalls, by ever-changing technologies and economies, and by evolving societal preferences--but it can be done. Economic valuations have been used in wetland priority rankings and in comparative investment analyses.

69. Turner, R. Kerry. 1988. "Wetland Conservation Economics and Ethics." Pp. 121-159 in *Economics, Growth and Sustainable Environments,* David Collard, David Pearce, and David Ulph, eds., St. Martin's Press, New York.
Discusses wetland function and structure values, option values, natural wetlands and substitutability, public decision making, environmental values, conservation vs. development, determinate cost benefit analysis vs. fixed standards approach, development values as the opportunity cost of wetland conservation, and environmental ethics.

70. Turner, R. K. 1991. "Project Planning and Sustainable Wetland Management." Pp. 103-109 in *Development Research: The Environmental Challenge,* J. T. Winpenny, ed., Overseas Development Institute, London.

71. Turner, R. K. 1991. "Economics and Wetland Management." *Ambio.* 20(2):59-63.
Stresses the urgent need for a balance to be struck between wetland conservation, sustainable utilization, and wetland conversion. The sustain-

able utilization and the maintenance of a sustainable flow of income derived from the wetlands stock is the key issue for developing economies. Economic valuation of the multi-functional wetland resource is required. Principles and methods used in the assessment of temperate wetlands in developed countries can aid the analysis of tropical wetlands in developing countries.

72. **Turner, R. K. 1992. "Policy Failures in Managing Wetlands." Pp. 9-43 in** *Market and Government Failures in Environmental Management: Wetlands and Forests,* **Organisation for Economic Co-operation and Development (OECD), Paris, France.**
Included in entry 206.

73. **Turner, R. Kerry. 1993.** *Sustainable Environmental Economics and Management: Principles and Practice.* **Belhaven Press, New York, 389 pp.**
Edited textbook with six chapters on principles, including one on the Contingent Valuation Method and another on Revealed Preference Methods. Five chapters on practice, including a section on tropical wetlands and irrigation development. Economic benefits are compared between floodplain and upstream development in Nigeria. Includes entry 21.

74. **U.S. Army Corps of Engineers, St. Paul District. 1988.** *The Minnesota Wetland Evaluation Methodology for the North Central United States.* **St. Paul District, U.S. Army Corps of Engineers, and Minnesota Wetland Evaluation Methodology Task Force, St. Paul, 97 pp.**
Developed to standardize evaluation of the functions, values, and characteristics of wetlands in the North Central U.S. The method is similar to the various Adamus methods and includes detailed technical evaluation of flood flow characteristics, water quality, wildlife, fish, shoreline anchoring, and visual values. A computerized version of WEM is also available.

75. **van der Valk, A. 1989. "Effective Wetlands Policy: Sticks or Carrots."** *Environmental Forum* **6(1):21-26.**
Compares and contrasts the so called swampbuster provision of the Food Security Act to the Conservation Reserve Program regarding wetland preservation and restoration. Endorses the establishment of a National Agricultural Wetlands Reserve Program primarily for water quality benefits. The wetlands selected for this type of program should have the highest potential for receiving agricultural runoff. Recommends further

study into effective wetland restoration and how well they function as environmental filters.

76. **van Kooten, G. C. 1993.** *Land Resource Economics and Sustainable Development: Economic Policies and the Common Good.* **Department of Agricultural Economics, University of British Columbia, Vancouver, British Columbia, 450 pp.**
Textbook on land use and the role of economic analysis.

77. **Ward, Kevin M. and John W. Duffield, eds. 1992.** *Natural Resource Damages: Law and Economics.* **John Wiley and Sons, Inc., Wiley Law Productions, New York, 684 pp.**
Contains three different parts which concentrate on analyzing some of the problems associated with environmental damages. Part I examines the legal basis for liability for natural resource damages in both theory and practice. Part II examines the economic perspective on these issues with regard to the welfare implications, valuation, revealed preference, contingent valuation, externalities, and public goods. Part III contains case studies of environmental damages. One of the case studies concentrates on assessing the damages of oil spills on estuaries and marshes. Another concentrates upon the economics of wetlands restoration. Includes entries 145 and 307.

78. **Whitehead, J. C. 1992.** "Measuring Use Value From Recreation Participation." *Southern Journal of Agricultural Economics* **24:113-119.**
Provides a method by which use value can be estimated solely from participation decision, rather than estimating conditional recreation participation probabilities and their intensity of use. The one-step resource valuation method allows estimation of use values from coefficients of the logistic regression recreation participation equation. The benefits of the model are the reduced data and effort required to value natural resource areas. Empirical estimates are presented of current and forecasted use values in an area of wetlands with potential surface coal mining in a western Kentucky coalfield.

79. **Williams, Michael, ed. 1991.** *Wetlands: A Threatened Landscape.* **Basil Blackwell, Inc., Cambridge, Massachusetts, 419 pp.**
Discusses three major areas of wetland science: (1) evolution, occurrence, and composition of wetlands and the physical and biological dynamics; (2) the impact of agriculture, industry, urbanization, and recreation; and (3) management and preservation of wetlands.

80. Willison, J. H. M., S. Bondrup-Nielsen, C. D. Drysdale, T. B. Herman, N. W. P. Munro, and T. L. Pollock, eds. 1992. *Science and the Management of Protected Areas.* Elsevier Science Publishing Co. Inc., New York, 548 pp.

WETLAND ECONOMICS, EMPIRICAL

OVERVIEW

This section includes mostly publications reporting dollar values for wetlands. In addition, some general values manuscripts are included to help provide a broader background of the values literature. There were probably as many empirical attempts to evaluate the dollar values of wetlands in the past five years than there were prior to that time. A 1989 bibliography (Leitch and Ekstrom 1989) identified fewer than 200 publications on economic valuation of wetlands. A few dozen, at most, authors had written more than one or two accounts of empirical wetland valuation prior to 1989. Then and now many more authors write about the need for economic valuations or the problems carrying out economic valuations than those who actually attempt to do empirical evaluations.

Some new names and locations have appeared in the literature reporting wetland values, including Whitehead (1993) in the U.S., Turner (1991) in the U.K., van Kooten (1993) and van Vuuren (1989) in Canada, and many others. The geographic range of wetland valuation literature included represents at least 25 states, 6 Canadian provinces, and 29 countries.

A key problem remaining with empirical evaluation is that while economists have the basic tools to evaluate wetlands, they lack the appropriate data from other disciplines necessary to operationalize them. Both economists and physical/biological scientists are to blame--economists for not communicating their data needs explicitly and physical/biological scientists for not fully appreciating the role of economics in policymaking. This section contains entries from academic journals to a limited number of special interest magazine articles which are included to demonstrate the range of printed sources of wetland evaluation discussions.

REFERENCES

Leitch, Jay A. and Brenda L. Ekstrom. 1989. *Wetland Economics and Assessment: An Annotated Bibliography.* Garland Publishing, Inc., New York.

Turner, R. Kerry. 1991. *Wetlands: Market and Intervention Failures, Four Case Studies.* Earthscan Publications Limited, London.

van Kooten, G. Cornelis. 1993. "Bioeconomic Evaluation of Government Agricultural Programs on Wetlands Conversion." *Land Economics* 69(1):27-38.

van Vuuren, Willem and Roy Pierre. 1989. "Economic Evaluation of Wetland Preservation." Pp. 229-234 in *Wetlands: Inertia or Momentum,* Michal J. Bardecki and Nancy Patterson, Federation of Ontario Naturalists, Don Mills, Ontario, Canada.

Whitehead, J. C. 1993. "Economic Valuation of Wetland Resources: A Review of the Value Estimates." *Journal of Environmental Systems* 22(2):151-161.

SELECTED BIBLIOGRAPHY

81. **Abt, Robert C. and William L. Finger. 1989. "Resource Policy in the Everglades Agricultural Area: A Historical and Economic Perspective."** *Journal of Environmental Management* **29(1):83-93.**

The state of Florida is currently considering options for reducing the environmental consequences of drainage and development encouraged by historical land-use policies. This paper puts the current land use situation in an historical context and examines the efficiency and equity implications of several policies. The interactions of state resource policy and national agricultural policy are shown to affect both the level and distribution of environmental costs. The implicit cost of current policy option is estimated.

82. **Adams, W. M. 1992.** *Wasting the Rain: Rivers, People, and Planning in Africa.* **University of Minnesota Press, Minneapolis, 256 pp.**
Provides an overview of African water resource development. Focuses particularly upon large scale projects which have failed and the reasons behind their failure. Includes a chapter on using Africa's wetlands describing several of the economic benefits that wetlands provide. Among those benefits are groundwater recharge, water supply, forage and hunting resources, wood resources, grazing, fish, and agricultural produce. Estimates quantities of some outputs but does not estimate monetary values.

83. Adams, W. M. 1993. "Indigenous Use of Wetlands and Sustainable Development in West Africa." *The Geographical Journal* 159(2): 209-218.
Discusses indigenous systems of water resource management and the implications of water resource development projects on the ecology and economy of wetlands in West Africa.

* Allen, Geoffrey P. and Thomas H. Stevens. 1983. *Use of Hedonic Price Technique to Evaluate Wetlands.*
Cited above as entry 3.

84. Amacher, G. S., R. J. Brazee, J. W. Bulkley, and R. W. Moll. 1989. *Application of Wetlands Valuation Techniques: Examples from Great Lakes Coastal Wetlands.* School of Natural Resources, University of Michigan, Ann Arbor, 38 pp.
Empirical study on Saginaw Bay wetlands. Methods include valuing environmental quality as an input, implicit price hedonics method, travel cost method, and two noneconomic methods; energy analysis and gross expenditure. Concludes that report is an improvement over previous work, but additional data collections are required to develop even more accurate methods. Recommends modifications of these valuation procedures to include more data, especially for commercial and recreational fishing.

85. Anderson, A. B. 1990. "Extraction and Forest Management by Rural Inhabitants in the Amazon Estuary." Pp. 65-85 in *Alternatives to Deforestation: Steps Towards Sustainable Use of the Amazon Rain Forest,* A. B. Anderson, ed., Columbia University Press, New York.
An account is given of the use of forest resources by descendants of Amerindians (caboclos or ribeirinhos) in floodplain forests of the Amazon estuary. Relatively high accessibility and high concentration of resources have made these forests an historical source of timber, edible fruits, fibers, latex, and medicines. Although the caboclos' use of these forests is usually viewed as mere extraction, it frequently involves subtle forms of management such as favoring highly desirable species and eliminating or thinning less desirable competitors, while maintaining the essential structure and composition of the forest. These practices are simple and inexpensive, and facilitate access to and exploitation of forest resources.

86. Anderson, A. B. and M. A. G. Jardim. 1989. "Costs and Benefits of Floodplain Forest Management by Rural Inhabitants in the Amazon Estuary: A Case Study of Acai Palm Production." Pp.

114-129 in *Fragile Lands of Latin America: Strategies for Sustainable Development*, J. O. Browder, ed., Westview Press, Boulder, Colorado.

A brief account is given of forests where acai palm (*Euterpe oleracea*, a multipurpose species producing a wide variety of market and subsistence products) occurs in the floodplain of the Amazon estuary, Brazil, and of the harvesting of both fruits and palm hearts. A field experiment was established to quantify the costs and benefits of managing native populations of acai. Results indicate that rational extraction of palm hearts does not reduce fruit harvest. Economic analysis indicated that the benefits outweigh the costs by $109.83/ha. Although this extensive form of forest management provides relatively low economic returns per unit area, it appears to be economically rational because of its low cost requirement, minimum risk, and apparent sustainability.

87. **Anderson, A. B. and E. M. Ioris. 1992. "Valuing the Rain Forest: Economic Strategies by Small-Scale Forest Extractivists in the Amazon Estuary."** *Human Ecology* 20(3):337-369.
Annual income and expenditure were measured of ten households on Combu Island, located in the Amazon estuary near the major port city of Belem; in addition, local uses and management of natural resources on the island were documented. Average annual income per household was less than $4,000, derived primarily from the harvest and sale of non-timber forest products. The results show that the combination of proximity to a major market and appropriate resource management can lead to high and apparently sustainable economic returns.

88. **Aust, W. M., S. F. Mader, L. J. Mitchell, and R. Lea. 1990. "An Approach to the Inventory of Forested Wetlands for Timber-Harvesting Impact Assessment."** *Forest Ecology Management* 33-34(1-4):215-225.
Assesses timber-harvesting impacts on tidal freshwater-palustrine wetlands in southwestern Alabama by providing relevant biophysical and socio-economic data to policy making agencies.

89. **Baker, Kimberly Anne, M. Siobhan Fennessy, and William J. Mitsch. 1991. "Designing Wetlands for Controlling Coal Mine Drainage: An Ecologic-Economic Modelling Approach."** *Ecological Economics* 3:1-24.
Develops a simulation model of the efficiency and economics of an application of ecotechnology--using a created wetland to receive and treat coal mine drainage. The model examines the role of loading rates of iron on treatment efficiencies and the economic costs of wetland versus

conventional treatment of mine drainage. It is calibrated with data from an Ohio wetland site and verified from multi-site data from Tennessee and Alabama. The model predicts that iron removal is closely tied to loading rates and that the cost of wetland treatment is less than that of conventional iron loading rates of approximately 20-25 g Fe m^{-2} day^{-1} and removal efficiencies less than 85 percent. A wetland to achieve these conditions would cost approximately $50,000 per year according to the model. When higher loading rates exist and higher efficiencies are needed, wetland systems are more costly than conventional treatment.

90. **Ball, J. P. 1990. "Influence of Subsequent Flooding Depth on Cattail Control by Burning and Mowing."** *Journal of Aquatic Plant Management* 28(Jan.):32-36.
Compared burning and mowing of cattail marshes in southern Ontario for increasing habitat for waterfowl. Found that mowing is preferable in shallow water, and burning does just as well in deeper water.

91. **Baltezore, James F., Jay A. Leitch, and William C. Nelson. 1987.** *Economic Analysis of Draining Wetlands in Kidder County, North Dakota.* **Agricultural Economics Report No. 230, Agricultural Experiment Station, North Dakota State University, Fargo, 58 pp.**
Estimates profitability of draining wetlands for agricultural production under various drainage costs and commodity prices. If a farmer receives government target or historic county average prices, draining some wetlands is economically feasible. Possible loss of government target prices and lower cash and future county average prices makes draining wetlands an irrational economic decision. Therefore, Swampbuster will be a disincentive to wetland drainage in North Dakota only as long as cash grain prices are low.

92. **Baltezore, James F., Jay A. Leitch, Sara F. Beekie, Preston F. Schutt, and Kevin L. Grosz. 1991.** *Status of Wetlands in North Dakota in 1990.* **Agricultural Economics Report No. 269, Agricultural Experiment Station, North Dakota State University, Fargo, 73 pp.**
Assesses status of North Dakota wetlands by evaluating the extent of protected and threatened wetlands. Discusses impacts of current state and federal legislation influencing wetland use. Found that threatened wetland acres in North Dakota will remain low as long as (1) agricultural commodity prices are low, (2) federal and state wetland legislation is maintained, and (3) wetland restoration programs are competitive with

private market incentives for drainage. Discusses wetland restoration in North Dakota under Conservation Reserve Program, Wetland Reserve Program, U.S. Fish and Wildlife Service, and other restoration programs.

93. **Barbier, E. B. 1989.** *Economic Evaluation of Tropical Wetland Resources: Applications in Central America.* **Report by the London Environmental Economics Center for Centro Agronomico Tropical de Investigation y Ensenaza (CATIE) and the IUCN Regional Wetlands Program, London.**

94. **Bardecki, Michal J. 1988.** *The Application of Willingness-to-Pay, Opportunity Cost, and Cumulative Impact Methods to Greenock Swamp, Ontario.* **Report 3 of** *Wetlands are not Wastelands,* **Sustainable Development Branch, Canadian Wildlife Service and Wildlife Habitat Canada, Ottawa, 122 pp.**
Identifies Greenock Swamp functions and evaluates them with willingness-to-pay, opportunity costs, and cumulative impact methods; also identifies weaknesses of each method. Found that the willingness-to-pay method produced results of little value, as there was evidently starting point bias, lack of knowledge of the study area, an inappropriate sampling frame, and an unsuitable questionnaire. Concludes that the opportunity cost method cannot be comprehensive for a number of reasons. Also concluded that a search for an identification of specific evaluation criteria remains the principal requisite for successful application of the cumulative impact approach. See entry 8.

95. **Bardecki, Michal J. 1989.** "Agriculture and Wetlands: An Update." **Pp. 255-277 in** *Wetlands: Inertia or Momentum,* **Michal J. Bardecki and Nancy Patterson, eds., Federation of Ontario Naturalists, Don Mills, Ontario, Canada.**
Reviews the nature and extent of recent drainage activity which has resulted in the loss of 55 to 95 percent of the wetlands in Ontario. Argues that the inclusion of drainage activities in the Environmental Assessment Act will prove ineffective in mitigating impacts on wetland areas. Recommends rational multi-objective planning for agricultural land drainage in the province. Included in entry 14.

96. **Bardecki, Michal J., E. W. Manning, and Wayne K. Bond. 1989.** "The Reality of Valuing Wetlands: The Case of Greenock Swamp, Ontario, Canada." **Pp. 81-90 in** *Wetlands: Concerns and Successes-Proceedings of a Symposium,* **David W. Fisk, ed., American Water Resources Association, Bethesda, Maryland.**

Evaluates and discusses the results of three different methods for valuing wetlands; the willingness-to-pay approach, the opportunity cost approach, and a cumulative assessment approach. Included in entry 33.

97. **Becker, R. H. 1989. "America's Wild and Scenic Rivers: The Dilemma of Protection--A Question of Values."** *The Station* **50:123-125. (Southeast Forest Experiment Station, Forest Service, U.S. Department of Agriculture, Asheville, North Carolina).**
Paper presented at the Symposium on the Forested Wetlands of the Southern United States, July 12-14, 1988, Orlando, Florida.

98. **Bedford, Barbara L. 1990. "Increasing the Scale of Analysis: The Challenge of Cumulative Impact Assessment for Great Lakes Wetlands." Pp. 186-195 in** *Wetlands of the Great Lakes: Protection and Restoration Policies--Status of the Science,* **Jon A. Kusler and Richard Smardon, eds., Proceedings of an International Symposium, Association of State Wetland Managers, Inc., Berne, New York.**
Presents the conceptual framework for resolving the incongruity of scale for wetlands of the Great Lakes. Argues that the primary need is for a shift upward in the level of assessment analysis. Discusses the various necessary elements for that shift: temporal and spatial boundaries, classification, information required, and a provisional set of goals for the entire wetland resource base of the Great Lakes. Included in entry 178.

99. **Beekie, Sara F. 1991.** *A Benefit-Cost Framework for Analyzing a Waterfowl Habitat Restoration.* **M.S. thesis, North Dakota State University, Fargo, 111 pp.**
Presents a benefit-cost framework that both economist and noneconomist can use to assess proposed public projects, such as waterfowl habitat restoration. The reclamation of Lake Christina in west central Minnesota was used as a case study. The *in situ* use values of the lake were monetarily quantified. The estimated B-C ratio for the reclamation project was 1.09:1, suggesting a positive net return to society.

100. **Bell, Frederick W. 1989.** *Application of Wetland Valuation Theory to Florida Fisheries.* **Department of Economics, Florida State University, Tallahassee, Florida, 118 pp.**
Evaluates, in economic terms, the value of estuarine wetlands to marine fisheries by valuing the willingness-to-pay for the marginal product of the fishing product. Found the value of an acre of wetland to contribute $35 annually to Florida fisheries.

* Bergstrom, John C., John Stoll, John P. Titre, and Vernon L. Wright. 1989. "Economic Value of Wetland-Based Recreation."
Cited above as entry 16.

* Bergstrom, John C. and John R. Stoll. 1989. "Recreational Benefits of Wetland Protection."
Cited above as entry 17.

101. Bergstrom, John and Richard Brazee. 1991. "Benefit Estimation." Pp. 18-22 in *A National Policy of "No Net Loss" of Wetlands: What do Agricultural Economists Have to Contribute?* Ralph E. Heimlich, ed., Staff Report No. AGES 9149, Resources and Technology Division, Economic Research Service, U.S. Department of Agriculture, Washington, D.C.
Discusses concerns and problems such as restriction of property rights, adequacy of the supply of wetlands and the issue of conservation vs. restoration with the economic valuation of wetlands as brought about by a policy of no-net-loss. Included in entry 153.

102. Berry, C. R., K. F. Higgins, and G. Krull. 1992. "Valuation of Hay and Bait Fish Harvested From Privately-Owned South Dakota Wetlands." Pp. 37-44 in *Proceedings of the South Dakota Academy of Science*, Department of Wildlife and Fisheries, South Dakota State University, Brookings.

103. Bhattacharyya, J. 1990. "Uses, Values, and Use Values of the Sundarbans." *Agriculture and Human Values* 7(2):34-39.
Decimation of the Sundarbans mangrove forests in Bangladesh and West Bengal, India, has resulted from attempts to satisfy short-term demands by exhausting the chances of satisfying future demands. The forest cannot be preserved by a policy that under-values the urgency of the short-term needs or by a policy that is imposed from above, but it may be by social forestry. Social forestry augments the supply of forest products from non-forest lands and, most significantly, includes the users in developing appropriate forest policies.

104. Boehlje, Michael D., Philip M. Raup, and Kent D. Olson. 1990. *Land Values and Environmental Regulation.* Staff paper presented at the Second Annual Conference on Agriculture and the Environment, Itasca State Park, Institute of Agriculture, Forestry and Home Economics, University of Minnesota, St. Paul, 25 pp.

Concludes that (1) increases in land values are because of decreased supply of unencumbered land and/or a truncation of the lower end of the price distribution, (2) regulations and policies to maintain and restore wetlands will lower the value of affected properties, and (3) the difference in value between environmentally benign and encumbered land will widen.

105. **BP Exploration (Alaska) Inc. 1989.** *Alaska Wetlands & Energy Development.* **Anchorage, Alaska, 28 pp.**
An industry account of Alaskan wetlands. Argues that permafrost wetlands are different, are almost entirely undisturbed, and that new policies should recognize those differences. Discusses mitigation of North Slope wetlands and what the no-net-loss concept means for Alaska.

106. **Brindell, J. R. 1988. "Balancing New Development with Conservation of Wetlands in Florida."** *Urban Law and Policy* **9(4):331-344.**

107. **Burling, James S. 1992. "Property Rights, Endangered Species, Wetlands, and Other Critters: Is it Against Nature to Pay for a Taking?"** *Land Water Law Review* **27(2):309-362.**

108. **Bush, George. 1990. "No Net Loss of Wetlands."** *Popular Science* **237(4):8, with adjoining editorial p. 9.**
President Bush's statement on the national value of wetlands, encouraging conservation and no-net-loss.

109. **Carey, Marc, Ralph Heimlich, and Richard Brazee. 1990.** *A Permanent Wetland Reserve: Analysis of a New Approach to Wetland Protection.* **Agricultural Information Bulletin Number 610, Economic Research Service, U.S. Department of Agriculture, Washington, D.C., 16 pp.**
Proposes a permanent wetland reserve program as the Swampbuster Provision of 1985 Farm Act and other acts may be insufficient to maintain no-net-loss in wetland acreage. Reviews the importance of wetlands, past and present federal policies, and dimensions of a reserve under three sizes. Analyzes the likely geographic distribution of the reserve and likely crop rotations affected. Estimates potential easement and restoration costs.

110. **Carney, Judith. 1993. "Converting Wetlands, Engendering the Environment: The Intersection of Gender with Agrarian Change in the Gambia."** *Economic Geography* **69(4):329-357.**

Examines how agricultural diversification and food security are transforming wetland environments in the Gambia. New irrigation schemes encouraged male household heads to enclose wetlands for private gain and wealth accumulation, thereby superseding the communal tenure systems prevalent in the lowland systems. This shift in agrarian relations in the Gambia has led to increased conflict between men and women over the distribution of work and the benefits experienced by increased household earnings.

111. **Caulfield, Jon, John Welker, and Ralph Meldahl. 1992.** *Opportunity Costs of Streamside Management Zones on an Industrial Forest Property.* **General Technical Report SO-93:639-644, U.S. Department of Agriculture, Washington, D.C.**

112. **Colby, B. G. 1991. "Economic Incentives and Agricultural Drainage Problems: The Role of Water Transfers." Pp. 803-820 in** *The Economics and Management of Water and Drainage in Agriculture,* **A. Dinar and D. Zilberman, eds., Kluwer Academic Publishers, Dordrecht, The Netherlands.**

113. **Colman, David R. 1989. "Economic Issues From the Broads Grazing Marshes Conservation Scheme (BGMCS)."** *Journal of Agricultural Economics* **40(3):336-344.**
Examines two key issues relating to the use of fixed-price conservational contracts of the type embodied in the new Environmentally Sensitive Area policy in the United Kingdom. The budgetary costs of the fixed-price contract are compared to those of (1) public purchase of land with leaseback for grazing, and (2) individual management agreements. Using a net present value criterion, public purchase emerges as the cheapest option, and management agreements as a superior option in defined circumstances. The paper also explores equity and efficiency issues arising from fixed price contracts. Concludes that for many farmers and landlords the fixed payment exceeded what was necessary to achieve the conservational objectives, while at the same time it was less than the profit foregone by farmers who might possibly have switched to arable farming.

114. **Cook, Ken. 1992. "Agriculture: Two Views."** *EPA Journal* **18(4):32-35.**
Recommends that state environmental agencies take a more active part in formulating environmental objectives for agriculture and ensuring that they are being practiced by farmers. Suggests that innovative ideas, such

as free market environmentalism, may provide better incentives to landowners, as they retain the rights to their property.

115. **Cooper, J. C. and J. Loomis. 1993. "Testing Whether Waterfowl Hunting Benefits Increase with Greater Water Deliveries to Wetlands."** *Environmental and Resource Economics* **3(6):545-561.**
The change in waterfowl hunting benefits due to an increase in water deliveries to the levels required for biologically optimal wildlife refuge management at California's San Joaquin Valley National Wildlife Refuges are estimated with the Travel Cost Method, using both ordinary least squares and Poisson count data estimators. To test whether these increases were statistically significant, the Krinsky and Robb technique was used to find confidence intervals around the consumers' surplus point estimates. The increases in consumers' surplus were found to be statistically significant in five of the six refuges based on OLS regression estimates and in all six refuges using Poisson count data regression estimates. In addition, a comparison of the marginal value of an acre-foot of water in consumptive recreational use versus agricultural use is made, with the finding that the marginal value of water in waterfowl hunting was greater than the marginal value of water in agriculture for one of the six refuges.

116. **Coreil, Paul D. 1993.** *Wetlands Functions and Values in Louisiana.* **Publication 2519, Louisiana Cooperative Extension Service, Louisiana State University Agricultural Center, Baton Rouge, 11 pp.**
Presents an overview of the functions Louisiana wetlands provide including consumer expenditures for many wetland-related goods or activities. Commercial uses of Louisiana wetlands include fisheries, forestry, furbearers, alligators, farming and ranching, and oil and natural gas. Recreational uses discussed are sport hunting and fishing, ecotourism, and cultural values. While dollar values of these activities are estimated, the portion attributable to the state's marshes and wetlands is not estimated. Intended for laypersons.

117. **Cosgrove, Denis and Geoff Petts. 1990.** *Water, Engineering and Landscape: Water Control and Landscape Transformation in the Modern Period.* **Belhaven Press, New York, 214 pp.**
Collection of essays, authored primarily by geographers, that address the development and management of the world's wetland environments. Includes examples from the U.K., the Sahara desert, Zimbabwe, Quebec, Wales, Venice, the Netherlands, the Danube River, and the U.S.

118. **Crandall, Kristine Birke. 1991.** *Measuring the Economic Benefits of Riparian Areas.* **M.S. thesis, The University of Arizona, 180 pp., (University Microfilms Inc., Order No: AAD13-45364).**
Applies nonmarket valuation tools (travel cost, contingent valuation, local economic impact assessment) to flowing streams and riparian ecosystems. Concludes that previously unmeasured wildlife viewing activities at Hassayampa River Preserve (Arizona) should be included in future water allocation decisions.

119. **Creel, M. and J. Loomis. 1992. "Recreation Value of Water to Wetlands in the San Joaquin Valley: Linked Multinomial Logit and Count Data Trip Frequency Models."** *Water Resources Research* **28(10):2597-2606.**
Recreational benefits from providing increased quantities of water to wildlife and fisheries habitats are estimated using linked multinomial logit site selection models and count data trip frequency models. The study encompasses waterfowl hunting, fishing, and wildlife viewing at 14 recreational resources in the San Joaquin Valley, California, including the National Wildlife Refuges, the State Wildlife Management Areas, and six river destinations. The economic benefits of increased water supplies to wildlife refuges were also examined by using the estimated models to predict changing patterns of site selection and overall participation due to increases in water allocations. Estimates of the dollar value per acre foot of water are calculated for increases in water to refuges. The resulting model is a flexible and useful tool for estimating the economic benefits of alternative water allocation policies for wildlife habitat and rivers.

* **Dalecki, M. G., J. C. Whitehead, and G. C. Bloomquist. 1993. "Sample Non-Response Bias and Aggregate Benefits in Contingent Valuation: An Examination of Early, Late, and Non-Respondents."**
Cited above as entry 28.

120. **Dalyell, Tam. 1990. "Wetlands Caught in the Tourist Trap."** *New Scientist* **128(1748):78.**
Discusses the environmental impacts of the construction of a beachside resort along the Coto Donana, Spain.

121. **Danielson, Leon E. 1989. "Changes in Wetlands Due to Agriculture."** **Pp. 18-24 in** *Alternative Perspectives on Wetland Evaluation and Use,* **E. Jane Luzar and Steven A. Henning, eds., SNREC Publication No. 27, Southern Rural Development Center, Mississippi State University, Mississippi State, 46 pp.**

Assesses the impact of agriculture incentive policies and programs, such as price and income support and the federal income tax code, on incentive to develop wetlands for agriculture in Washington County, North Carolina. A separate analysis was conducted to estimate similar incentives to convert pocosin wetlands to forestry. Found that the after-tax returns to land, labor, management, risk, and overhead from clearing and draining pocosin wetlands were relatively low based on the assumption and results of the analysis. Annualized net returns with which to pay for these cost factors ranged from $26 to $64. Concludes that already drained pocosins can provide sufficient returns to cover costs but the economic returns to clearing and draining at present may be sufficiently low so as to provide little economic incentive to clear and drain more North Carolina wetlands. Included in entry 192.

122. **Danielson, Leon. E., L. K. Gantt, and R. E. Noffsinger. 1988. "Economic Incentives to Clear and Drain Pocosin Wetlands." Pp. 791-800 in *Proceedings of the Symposium on Coastal Water Resources*, W. L. Lyke and T. J. Hovan, eds., Technical Publication, American Water Resources Association, Bethesda, Maryland.**
Presents the results of an analysis of the effects of selected federal programs on the rate of return to clearing and draining pocosin wetlands for growing crops. Programs analyzed include agricultural price and income supports, capital gains exclusion, expensing options for clearing and draining costs, and investment tax credit. Results suggest that these programs have a substantial but differential impact upon the incentives to clear and drain wetlands and that other conditions such as the productivity of the land and landowner characteristics also affect conversion incentives.

123. **Danielson, Leon E. and Rick A. Hamilton. 1989. "The Impact of Tax and Reforestation Incentives on Net Returns from Pocosin Development for Silviculture." *Wetlands* 9(1):1-12.**
Federal and state reforestation cost-share and income tax programs increase the economic incentives to grow timber, including production on pocosin wetlands that must be cleared and drained before planting. Elimination of the capital gains exclusion by the 1986 Tax Reform Act is estimated to reduce by 26 percent the rate of return to clearing and draining pocosin wetlands for timber production. The simulated loss of reforestation cost-share would reduce the rate of return by about 16 percent, while loss of investment tax credit and cost amortization tax incentives would reduce the rate of return by 20 percent. Removing all three programs simultaneously is estimated to reduce the rate of return by

48 percent. Several other factors influence the rate of return, including the amount of marketable timber on the tract at the time of clearing, the cost of ditching and draining, the productivity of the land, timber prices, and the marginal tax rate of the producer.

124. **Dennison, Mark S. and James F. Berry. 1993. *Wetlands: Guide to Science, Law, and Technology.* Noyes Publications, Park Ridge, New Jersey, 439 pp.**
Discusses wetland history, functions, and values within the context of federal, state, and local wetland protection laws, and presents the latest technological methodology for understanding the complexities of the issues. The book covers a variety of wetlands topics including ecological principles of wetland ecosystems, wetland types and how to recognize them, the relevant regulatory framework, mitigation, risk assessment to ecological resources, and restoration and creation.

125. **Dillman, Buddy L., Lawrence J. Beran, and Donal D. Hook. 1993. *Nonmarket Valuation of Freshwater Wetlands: The Francis Biedler Forest.* Report 135, South Carolina Water Resources Research Institute, Clemson University, 47 pp.**
Utilizes contingent valuation (CV) method to estimate the public willingness-to-pay (WTP) for the purchase of wetlands having different functional characteristics to be added to a South Carolina wetland preserve, the Francis Beidler Forest. The dichotomous choice version of the model was used to elicit the WTP of a statewide sample of 3,600 randomly selected households. Three types of adjacent wetlands which could be purchased were described: (1) frequently flooded bottomland typified by cypress-tupelo swamp, (2) infrequently flooded bottomland hardwood forest, and (3) nonbottomland pine plantation with hardwood runners. A 21 percent return of usable questionnaires was received. The different formulations of the statistical model produced mean estimates of household WTP between about $8 and $20. Household income and the size of the contribution requested were statistically significant. Also, respondents who were members of environmental organizations were different from others in their WTP and were more interested in preserving the non-bottomland pine plantation type wetlands.

126. **Doss, Cheryl R. and Steven J. Taff. 1993. "The Relationship of Property Values and Wetlands Proximity in Ramsey County, Minnesota." Paper presented at the Symposium on *Economics of Wetlands Preservation on Agricultural Land in Western Canada*, Department of Agricultural and Applied Economics, University of Minnesota, St. Paul, 42 pp.**

Using regression models, investigates and finds that the proximity to a wetland and the type of wetland influences nearby property values. Demonstrates how scrub-shrub and open water wetlands rank higher than emergent vegetation and forested wetlands.

127. **Dougherty, Steven T. 1989. "Evaluation of the Applicability of the Wetland Evaluation Technique (WET) to High Elevation Wetlands in Colorado."** Pp. 415-427 in *Wetlands: Concerns and Successes--Proceedings of a Symposium,* **David W. Fisk, ed., American Water Resources Association, Bethesda, Maryland.**
Found that WET (Adamus et al. 1987) is difficult to apply to two case studies in Colorado due to the lack of an extensive literature/data base for the region as well as questions that do not integrate regional considerations. Included in entry 33.

* **Douglas, Aaron J. 1989.** *Annotated Bibliography of Economic Literature on Wetlands.*
Cited above as entry 31.

128. **Douglas, Aaron J. and Richard L. Johnson. 1994. "Drainage Investment and Wetlands Loss: An Analysis of the Resources Inventory Data."** *Journal of Environmental Management* **40(4):341-355.**
Analyzes data gathered by the National Resources Inventory (NRI) in 1982 and 1987 to examine empirically the factors that generate wetland loss in the U.S. The cross-section regression models use the quantity of wetlands, the stock of drainage capital, the realty value of farmland, and drainage costs to explain most of the cross-state variation in wetland loss rates. Wetlands preservation efforts by federal agencies assume that pecuniary economic factors play a decisive role in wetland drainage. The empirical models tested in the paper validate this assumption.

129. **Dries, I. 1989.** *Development of Wetlands in Sierra Leone: Farmer's Rationality Opposed to Government Policy.* **ICRA Bulletin No. 29, International Centre for Development Oriented Research in Agriculture (ICRA), Wageningen, The Netherlands, 10 pp.**

130. **Dryer, Pam. 1992. "Wetlands vs. Agriculture."** *The Oxbow* **12(1):16-19.**
Reviews the battles and compromises between wildlife and agricultural interests since 1967 over wetland protection in North Dakota.

131. **Dugan, P. J. 1989. "Managing Wetlands for Sustainable Development."** Pp. 339-347 in *Nature Management and Sustainable*

Development, W. D. Verwey, ed., IOS, IUCN, Amsterdam, The Netherlands.

Discusses why wetlands are being lost to human society, and how environmentally sound management of wetlands can be achieved. While the world's wetlands are being lost as a result of drainage, poldering, damming and diversion of river water, point and non-point pollution, and increased demographic pressure leading to overgrazing and overfishing, the origin of most of these problems lies in four specific points: (1) poor understanding of the natural value of wetland ecosystems, (2) inaccurate predictions of the benefits from wetland conversion, (3) poor understanding of the fragility of wetland systems, and (4) lack of adequate management structures. If conservation is to be seen as positive and helpful to development, rather than negative and preservationist, the conservation community will need to invest more in integrated rural development activities which demonstrate how sustainable development can be achieved by means of environmentally sound management of wetland resources. Accordingly, much of the increasing investment in wetland conservation in the developing world is today being placed upon the development of management by which rural people can more effectively plan long-term strategies for wetland use, and have the economic flexibility to do so. This is illustrated by a case study from the inner Niger delta in Mali.

132.   Eargle, M. Frances and John Mark Dean. 1989. "A Functional Comparison of Two Bottomland Hardwood Sites in South Carolina Using WET." Pp. 372-380 in *Wetlands and River Corridor Management: Proceedings of an International Symposium*, Jon A. Kusler and Sally Daly, eds., Association of Wetland Managers, Inc., Omnipress, Madison, Wisconsin.

Tests the Wetland Evaluation Technique (WET) model for scientific efficacy for use among a sub-set of a complex system of wetlands. Then tested for reproducibility among investigators with diverse backgrounds. Included in entry 177.

133.   Ellanna, Linda J. and Polly C. Wheeler. 1989. "Wetlands and Subsistence-Based Economies in Alaska." *Arctic and Alpine Research* 21(4):329340.

Provides comparative examples to demonstrate that rural wetlands cannot be assumed to be unused. In fact, the uses of wetland habitats and resources by rural Alaskan Natives are subject to serious threat as a result of changing land status over the past few decades.

134.   Elliot, Lynne and George Mulamoottil. 1992. "Agricultural and Marsh Land Uses on Walpole Island: Profit Comparisons."

Canadian Water Resources Journal 17(2):111-119.
Presents a financial perspective in support of wetland preservation from a case study of the wetlands of Walpole Island, southwestern Ontario. The estimated average net operating profit for one hectare of wetlands on the island is $168.52 annually, while the weighted average net operating profit for one hectare of drained, agricultural land is $135.92 annually.

135. **Ellsworth, John C. 1988. "Assessing Wetland Visual Quality: Comparative Approaches and Management Implications." Pp. 97-103 in *Proceedings of the National Wetland Symposium: Urban Wetlands*, Jon A. Kusler, Sally Daly, and Gail Brooks, eds., Association of Wetland Managers, Inc., Berne, New York.**
Investigates the relationship of preference to two approaches to visual assessment: the descriptive inventory approach at various scales, and the perceptual preference approach. Included in entry 48.

136. **Ewel, K. C. 1990. "Multiple Demands of Wetlands." *BioScience* 40(9):660-665.**
Discusses functions of cypress wetlands and how the demand for these functions can be managed according to their compatibility.

137. **Feierabend, J. Scott. 1990. "Turnips, Carrots and Wetlands: Promoting Private Sector's Stewardship of a Public Sector Resource." Pp. 33-37 in *Income Opportunities for the Private Landowner through Management of Natural Resources and Recreational Access*, William N. Grafton, Anthony Ferrise, Dale Colyer, Dennis K. Smith, and James E. Miller, eds., R.D. No. 740, West Virginia University Extension Sevice, Morgantown.**
Methods of protecting wetlands are presented, such as subsidies and transferable development rights. A case study of Mississippi farmer attitudes toward waterfowl management is discussed. Included in item 142.

138. **Ferguson, Alan, Gary Holman, and Ron Kistritz. 1989. *Application of Wetland Evaluation Methods to the Cowichan Estuary, British Columbia*. Report 4 of *Wetlands are not Wastelands*, Sustainable Development Branch, Canadian Wildlife Service and Wildlife Habitat Canada, Ottawa, 94 pp.**
Identifies functions of the Cowichan Estuary and evaluates them with willingness-to-pay, opportunity cost, and cumulative impact methods. The total resource value attributable to the functions of the estuary is estimated at $55.6 million in present value terms ($114,000/hectare). See also entry 8.

139. Folke, C. 1991. "The Societal Value of Wetland Life-support." Ch. 1:141-171 in *The Series Analytic: Linking the Natural Environment and the Economy: Essays from the Eco-Eco Group*, C. Folke and T. Kåberger, eds., Kluwer Academic Publishers, Boston.
Analyzes the societal value of a Swedish wetland system with respect to the various economic functions such as cleansing nutrients and pollutants, maintaining the level and quality of drinking water, processing sewage, filtering coastal waters, sustaining genetic diversity, and preserving endangered species. Evaluates wetland conversion in terms of reduced solar energy fixing ability and the deterioration of the stored peat, and compares it to the cost of replacement in monetary and industrial energy terms.

* Gan, Christopher E. and E. Jane Luzar. 1993. "Conjoint Analysis of Wetland-Based Recreation Activities."
Cited above as entry 34.

140. Gersib, Richard A., Betty Elder, Kenneth F. Dinan, and Thomas H. Hupf. 1989. *Waterfowl Values by Wetland Type Within Rainwater Basin Wetlands with Special Emphasis on Activity Time Budget and Census Data.* Nebraska Game and Parks Commission and U.S. Fish and Wildlife Service, Lincoln, 105 pp.
Brings to light the critical importance of the Rainwater Basin area of Nebraska to waterfowl using the central flyway. Stresses the collective value of temporary, seasonal, and semipermanent wetlands as a dynamic system which must be maintained as a vital natural resource. Lauds the U.S. Environmental Protection Agency regulatory program as an important initiative but recommends the restoration of destroyed or highly degraded wetlands in order to insure adequate migratory waterfowl habitat in the central U.S.

141. Gopal, B. 1991. "Wetland (Mis)management by Keeping People Out: Two Examples from India." *Landscape Urban Ecology* 20(1-3):53-59.
Current emphasis on wetland management has two objectives: firstly, to conserve biotic diversity and representative habitats for their natural functions, and secondly, to maximize gains. Keoladeo Ghana National Park (at Bharatpur near Agra), well-known for its avifauna, and Lake Kolleru wetland (east coast of India) exemplify the two management objectives, respectively. Recent management practices in both wetlands have resulted, for example, in new problems as important as those the management initially sought to solve.

142. Grafton, William N., Anthony Ferrise, Dale Colyer, Dennis K. Smith, and James E. Miller, eds. 1990. *Income Opportunities for the Private Landowner Through Management of Natural Resources and Recreational Access.* R.D. No. 740, West Virginia University Extension Sevice, Morgantown, 414 pp.
Conference proceedings containing 44 papers in eight areas, many related to potential income sources from wetland resources. Includes entries 137 and 228.

143. Gray, Jerry. 1992. "Tax Judge Lowers Assessment of Undeveloped Wetlands Tract." *The New York Times*, 141(May 1):B5(L), col. 2., 12 col.
Owners of an undeveloped 240-acre wetland area in New Jersey, which lies near Giants Stadium, were able to lower the tax assessment of the land from $20 million to $1 million. The ruling was possible because of federal and state regulations that restrict the development of wetlands.

144. Griffith, J. A. and P. L. Jackson. 1990. *A Practical Assessment of the Wetland Evaluation Technique (WET) as a Tool for Meeting Oregon's Land Use Planning Goal Five Requirements.* 63rd Annual Meeting, Northwest Science Association, Corvallis, Oregon.
Discusses the use of the Wetland Evaluation Technique (WET) as a practical, rapid assessment methodology for meeting policy directives set forth in Oregon's LCDC Goal 5 concerning natural area inventory and analysis. Focuses on the issue of practicability from the standpoint of time, manpower, and the relative value of the results obtained from WET. Concludes from a case study which evaluated a wetland near Corvallis that WET produces wetland significance values comparable to other methods requiring greater time and expertise. But to continue the analysis beyond the first level would require greater time and expertise and therefore may pose problems to counties with large numbers of wetlands.

145. Grigalunas, Thomas A., James J. Opaluch, Deborah P. French, and Mark Reed. 1992. "Validating a Type A Assessment Model." Pp. 471-491 in *Natural Resource Damages: Law and Economics*, Kevin M. Ward and John W. Duffield, eds., John Wiley and Sons, Inc., Wiley Law Publications, New York.
Uses the National Resource Damage Assessment Model for coastal and marine environments to estimate the value of a Louisiana coastal wetland to be $1,892 per hectare. Included in entry 77.

146. Grosz, Kevin L. and Jay A. Leitch. 1990. "North Dakota House-holds' Attitudes Towards Wetlands." *Prairie Naturalist* 22(3): 201-206.

Surveyed 300 North Dakota households to assess their attitudes towards wetland protection, wetland values, and wetland literacy. Water quality, flood control, and education were identified as important wetland values. North Dakota residents were willing to provide wetland protection, even though knowledge about wetlands was low. A trade-off context is shown to result in different attitudes than valuations of wetlands in isolation.

147. Hall, H. Dale and Victor W. Lambou. 1989. "Determining the Value of Bottomland Hardwood Riverine Wetlands to Fisheries." In *Wetlands and River Corridor Management: Proceedings of an International Symposium*, Jon A. Kusler and Sally Daly, eds., Association of Wetland Managers, Inc., Omnipress, Madison, Wisconsin.

Summarizes the findings of the Fisheries Work-groups at the three Bottomland Hardwood (BLH) Workshops sponsored by the U.S. Environmental Protection Agency. Topics include (1) field evaluations of BLH sites, (2) permanent-water habitat, (3) access, (4) flood regime, (5) water quality, and (6) floodplain habitat. Included in entry 177.

148. Harbor, Jonathan M. 1994. "A Practical Method for Estimating the Impact of Land-use Change on Surface Runoff, Groundwater Recharge and Wetland Hydrology." *Journal of the American Planning Association* 60(1):95-103.

Uses readily available data in a simple spreadsheet analysis to estimate the impacts of land-use change on groundwater recharge, water supply, and wetland hydrology. Potential applications are plan review, raising community awareness of potential problems and support for regulatory action, and as part of local guidelines to minimize disturbance of the hydrological regime.

149. Harrison, George. 1989. "Prairie Potholes: What Are They and Why Is There Such a Hue and Cry Over Their Destruction?" *Sports Afield* 202(1):55-57.

Bemoans the current trend of prairie pothole loss from agriculture as a loss of habitat for ducks and other animals.

150. Hazeltine, William. 1992. "The Health Risks of Wetlands: The Western U.S. Perspectives." Pp. 781-791 in *Rational Readings*

on Environmental Concerns, Jay H. Lehr, ed., Van Nostrand Reinhold, New York.
Discusses the disease vectoring species associated with wetlands, mosquitoes in particular. Claims that the health issues surrounding encephalitis and malaria should not be ignored when making wetland management decisions.

151. Heimlich, R. E. 1989. "Changes in Wetlands Due to Urbanization: A Regional Perspective." Pp. 7-17 in *Alternative Perspectives on Wetland Evaluation and Use,* E. Jane Luzar and Steven A. Henning, eds., SNREC Publication No. 27, Southern Rural Development Center, Mississippi State University, Mississippi State.
Studies the conversion of wetlands to other uses in the Southeast U.S. from approximately 1970 to 1980. Compares the 10 percent wetland loss to urbanization and the 90 percent loss to agriculture. Concludes that urbanization is the most important driver behind wetland conversion in rapidly growing areas. Passes through an intermediate step of agriculture. Recommends a coordinated policy which would retain agricultural land and wetland protection must be integrated with urban growth. Included in entry 192.

152. Heimlich, Ralph E. 1989. "The Swampbuster Provision: An *A Priori* Evaluation of Effectiveness." Pp. 500-521 in *Wetlands: Concerns and Successes--Proceedings of a Symposium,* David W. Fisk, ed., American Water Resources Association, Bethesda, Maryland.
Analyzes the location and conversion probability of wetlands in relation to direct government payments from agricultural programs for U.S. counties. Concludes that areas with higher dependence on farm programs will be affected the most, such as Nebraska's Rainwater Basin, the Prairie Pothole Region of the Dakotas and Minnesota, and the Lower Mississippi Alluvial Plain. Wetland conversion in much of the Southern Coastal Plain, Florida, Michigan, and parts of the Klamath Basin will likely not be affected by withholding farm program benefits. The swampbuster act withholds a menu of farm program payments to farmers who convert wetlands. Included in entry 33.

153. Heimlich, Ralph E., ed. 1991. *A National Policy of "No Net Loss" of Wetlands: What do Agricultural Economists Have to Contribute?* Staff Report No. AGES 9149, Resources and Technology Division, Economic Research Service, U.S. Department of Agriculture, Washington, D.C., 40 pp.

Symposium proceedings explore how no-net-loss might operate and the economist's role in acquiring public rights of wetlands. Discusses valuing wetland benefits and alternatives to existing institutional mechanisms for controlling wetland loss. Includes entries 63, 101, 153, 324, and 330.

154.　**Heimlich, Ralph E. 1991. "Wetlands and Agriculture: New Relationships."** *Forum for Applied Research and Public Policy* **Spring:78-83.**

Provides an overview of public issues surrounding methods and assesses the impact of the Swampbuster Provision of the Food Security Act of 1985.

155.　**Heimlich, Ralph E. and Marlow Vesterby. 1989. "Conversion of Wetlands to Urban Uses: Evidence from Southeastern Counties."** **Pp. 161-173 in** *Wetlands: Concerns and Successes-- Proceedings of a Symposium,* **David W. Fisk, ed., American Water Resources Association, Bethesda, Maryland.**

Changes in land use on 5 million wetland acres were inventoried in a study of 68 Southeastern counties experiencing rapid population growth during the 1970s. Direct conversion to urban uses accounted for 30 percent of wetland losses, but wetlands made up only 10 percent of the land urbanized. Forty-four percent of wetlands converted were used for agriculture and rangelands, while 20 percent were converted to forest land. Regionally, 86 percent of wetlands in fast-growth counties are in the Southeast and 85 percent of gross wetland conversion occurs there. Included in entry 33.

156.　**Hickman, C. A. 1990. "Forested-Wetland Trends in the United States: An Economic Perspective."** *Forest Ecology and Management* **33-34(1-4):227-238.**

Forested wetlands provide habitat for a wide variety of fish and wildlife, play a role in flood control, have a positive effect on water quality, serve as the setting for many forms of outdoor recreation, and are a source of various commercially important products such as timber. In spite of these numerous benefits, however, the area of such lands in the U.S. has decreased substantially. To a large degree, these wetland losses have resulted from differing public and private perspectives of the benefits and costs associated with retaining such lands as opposed to converting them to other uses. Past public policies, particularly at the federal level, have also tended to encourage wetlands development. In looking to the future, several factors seem to suggest that further forested-wetland losses will be curtailed.

157. **Hollis, G. E., M. M. Holland, E. Maltby, and J. S. Larson. 1988. "Wise Use of Wetlands."** *Nature and Resources* **24(1):2-13.**
Highlights the functions and values of wetlands and explains how "wise use" can contribute to their sustainable utilization. Defines "wise use" and how the term has developed in the Ramsar Convention and Unesco Biosphere Reserves Program. Provides case studies of "wise use" including: A River Basin Approach to Biosphere Reserve Management, Manu, Peru; The Master Plan for Water Resources in Norway; A Local Management Plan for Panbros Lagoon, near Accra, Ghana; National Inventories of Wetlands in New Zealand; and A Legislative Approach Through the Federal Laws of the U.S.

158. **Hotinga, F., H. Peters, and S. Zanen. 1991. "Potentials of Bas-fonds in Agropastoral Development in Sanmatenga, Burkina Faso."** Part 3B in *Wetlands in Drylands: The Agroecology of Savanna Systems in Africa*, **I. Scoones, ed., International Institute for Environmental Development, London, 14 pp.**
Examines the physical, social, and economic factors affecting the development of bas-fonds valleys in Sanmatenga Province, Burkina Faso, presenting appropriate alternatives to large dams with downstream development. Individual bas-fonds development will increase crop yields in the short term, although regional coordination will be required to combine technical intervention with improved land management practices, for long term yield improvements.

159. **Hovde, Brett. 1993.** *Dollar Values of Two Prairie Potholes.* **M.S. thesis, North Dakota State University, Fargo, 91 pp.**
Dollar values were estimated for one seasonal wetland and one semipermanent wetland located in North Dakota. Attributes of wetlands lead to functions, functions to outputs, and outputs to economic values, based on site-specific considerations. Assessing the values of these wetlands' outputs required careful consideration of the ecological values and the societal values. Each wetland's total value was estimated by aggregating the values of its compatible outputs. The values found for specific outputs and total values varied between the two study wetlands. The Nome wetland's estimated annual value to society is $16 per acre or $282 per acre when capitalized for 30 years at 4 percent. The Buchanan wetland's estimated annual value to society is $12 per acre or $261 per acre when capitalized for 60 years at 4 percent. The owner of the Nome wetland could expect to receive $12 ($4 per acre) annually from the Nome wetland. The annual owner value of the Buchanan wetland is $77 ($5 per acre). The dearth of applicable physical-biological science

information necessitated many assumptions, which represent areas of needed research.

160. Hovde, Brett and Jay A. Leitch. 1994. *Valuing Prairie Potholes: Five Case Studies.* Agricultural Economics Report No. 319, Agricultural Experiment Station, North Dakota State University, Fargo, 27 pp.

Dollar values were estimated for four individual prairie potholes and a wetland complex located in North Dakota. Assessments of value were made from four perspectives: owner, user, regional, and social. Values of specific outputs and total values varied among the five study sites. Annual per acre values varied from the $4 owner value for the Nome wetland to the $373 regional value for the Alice wetland. The dearth of applicable physical-biological science information necessitated many assumptions, which represent areas of needed research. The social values estimated in this study are appropriate only for social decisions about the use or condition of the study's specific wetlands.

161. Hovde, Brett and Jay A. Leitch. 1994. "Empirical Valuation of Prairie Wetlands: Five Case Studies." Pp. 195-207 in *Water: A Resource in Transition--Proceedings of the 47th Annual Conference, Canadian Water Resources Association,* Winnipeg, Manitoba, June 14-17, 1994.

A summary of entry 160.

162. Hubbard, Daniel E. 1988. *Glaciated Prairie Wetland Functions and Values: A Synthesis of the Literature.* Biological Report 88(43), U.S. Department of the Interior, Fish and Wildlife Service and South Dakota Cooperative Fish and Wildlife Research Unit, Washington, D.C., 50 pp.

163. Hubbard, Daniel E. 1989. *Wetland Values in the Prairie Pothole Region of Minnesota and the Dakotas.* Department of Wildlife and Fisheries Sciences, South Dakota State University, Brookings, 65 pp.

Assigns per acre values to wetland functions in South Dakota: faunal functional support, recreational hunting, forage value, hydrological, floral functional support, and nutrient and sediment retention. Found values for hunting to range from $487 per acre for private wetlands in the eastern region of the state to $1,020.51 per acre for public wetlands in the western region. Estimated annual values of nonconsumptive uses for muskrat trapping ($0-$59.25 per acre), bait production of fathead minnows ($0-$46.54 per acre), and tiger salamanders ($0-$762.72 per acre). Estimated the annual value of wetland hay production for three different types of wetlands: temporary ($27.23-$81.69 per acre), seasonal ($0-149.77 per acre), and semipermanent ($0-$177 per acre). Assigns an unknown, but existing, value to other wetland functions such as nonresident hunting, nonconsumptive recreation, recreational trapping, other specie pelts (besides muskrats), water retention, nutrient/sediment retention, and water table maintenance.

164. **Hubbard, Daniel E. 1988.** *Forage Potential of Seasonal Wetlands.* **Ph.D. thesis, South Dakota State University, Brookings, 181 pp. (University Microfilms Inc., Order No.: DA8823753).**
Vegetation in six seasonal wetland communities was assessed for its nutritional value. On an area basis, seasonal wetland basins produce higher standing crops of forage than uplands in a native mixed-grass prairie situation. However, nutritional value is sensitive to native species composition and time during the growing season it is assessed.

165. **Jennings, Simon. 1992.** "Potential Effects of Estuarine Development on the Success of Management Strategies for the British Bass Fishery." *Ambio* 21(7):468-470.
Bass, a highly prized sport and table fish in England and Wales, are being rapidly depleted. The article identifies two different reasons for the depletion of fishery resources: overexploitation and development. Development of estuaries results in a loss of nursery habitat for juvenile bass. Development can occur in four different ways: (1) claiming new land for industry, waste disposal, or recreation; (2) construction of barrages to create recreational lakes; (3) pollution; and (4) power station. Concludes that it is critical that the amount of nursery habitat to be preserved for bass should be determined.

166. **Josephson, R. M. 1992.** *An Economic Evaluation of Land Use Changes in Southwest Manitoba: A Report to the Manitoba Habitat Heritage Corporation.* **Department of Agricultural Economics and Farm Management, University of Manitoba, Winnipeg, Canada, 51 pp.**
Reports on a survey of 80 farmers known to have adopted land use modifications. Land use modifications analyzed included permanent cover set asides, rotational grazing, zero till, minimum till, chemical fallow, green manure fallow, inter-pothole seeding, upland forage, and delayed cut forage. An average additional net income of $13.27 per acre per year was realized.

167. **Kahn F. 1991. "Palms as Key Swamp Forest Resources in Amazonia."** *Forest Ecology and Management* **38(3-4):133-142.**
Native palms provide many useful products, and have a significant place in the daily life of most inhabitants of Amazonia. Found that the most economically valuable types of palms stand in swampy areas which have soil unsuitable for agriculture.

168. **Kangas, P. C. 1990. "Long-Term Development of Forested Wetlands."** Pp. **25-51** in *Ecosystems of the World 15: Forested Wetlands,* **Elsevier Science Publishing Co., New York.**
Concepts and models of wetland development are reviewed. Uses energy value concept to value and identify landscapes. Concludes that aspects of ecosystem and landform develop together in a wetland landscape. Included in entry 52.

169. **Kantrud, Harold A., Gary L. Krapu, and George A. Swanson. 1989.** *Prairie Basin Wetlands of the Dakotas: A Community Profile.* **Biology Report, 85(7.28), U.S. Fish and Wildlife Service, Washington, D.C., 116 pp.**
Outlines the wetland subsystems, classes, and subclasses that occur in the Prairie Pothole Region. Provides useful reference to their geologic, climactic, hydrologic, biotic, and ecological setting. Includes a chapter on the subject of human uses and impacts to the region's wetlands, highlighting the economic functions, wetland ownership, wetland degradation, drainage management and restoration, and future prospects. Some of the human uses and impacts discussed include recreational benefits (such as in waterfowl), wetland ownership, wetland degradation and drainage, wetland management, and wetland restoration.

170. **Kent, Donald M. 1994.** *Applied Wetlands Science and Technology.* **Lewis Publishers, Boca Raton, Florida, 400 pp.**
Comprehensive guide useful for those involved with wetland function, protection, and management. Provides fundamentals for defining and regulating wetlands, as well as identifying and delineating wetlands. Functions and values, ecological assessment, and how to minimize impacts are covered in depth.

* **Kiker, Clyde F. and Gary Lynne. 1989. "Can Mama Help? Multiple Alternative/Multiple Attribute Evaluation of Wetlands.**
Cited above as entry 43.

171. **Kimmage, K. and W. M. Adams. 1992. "Wetland Agriculture Production and River Basin Development in the Hadejia-**

Jama'are Valley, Nigeria." *The Geographical Journal* 158(1):1-12.
Describes the nature and magnitude of agricultural production in the floodplain wetland of the Hadejia-Jama'are rivers in northern Nigeria. Most of the agricultural production is dependent on the annual flood, which has been reduced in magnitude by drought, dam construction, and water abstraction for irrigation upstream. The economic importance of the floodplain is placed in the context of the performance of the costly formal large-scale irrigation schemes upstream which have been favored by the river basin planning process.

172. Knutson, Melinda G., Donald J. Leopold, and Richard C. Smardon. 1990. "Assessing the Visual Quality of Small Islands and Shoals in the Thousand Islands Region." Pp. 166-175 in *Wetlands of the Great Lakes: Protection and Restoration Policies--Status of the Science*, Jon A. Kusler and Richard Smardon, eds., Association of State Wetland Managers, Inc., Berne, New York.
Assesses the visual qualities of island and shoal resources. Recommends to protect undeveloped islands and shoals less than 0.8 ha in size using existing laws, purchase agreements, conservation easements, and public education. Included in entry 178.

173. Kokwe, M. 1991. "The Role of Dambos in Agricultural Development in Zambia." Part 3E in *Wetlands in Drylands: The Agroecology of Savanna Systems in Africa*, I. Scoones, ed., International Institute for Environmental Development, London, 35 pp.
Reviews the role of patchy wetlands in agricultural development in Zambia. The economic value of wetlands for agriculture and gardening, fishing, livestock production, water supplies, and wild products is addressed.

174. Kolawole, A. 1991. "Economics and Management of Fadama in Northern Nigeria." Part 3A in *Wetlands in Drylands: The Agroecology of Savanna Systems in Africa*, I. Scoones, ed., International Institute for Environmental Development, London, 28 pp.
Examines the role of wetland farming in environmental resource management on four sites. A general section on definition and typology of wetlands in Nigeria is followed by the case studies and a final section on socioeconomic decisions in fadama management. In addition to farming, the fadama were found to be invaluable for livestock grazing and a source of famine foods in periods of environmental stress.

175. **Kramer, Randall A. and Leonard Shabman. 1993. "The Effects of Agriculture and Tax Policy Reform on the Economic Return to Wetland Drainage in the Mississippi Delta Region."** *Land Economics* 69(3):249-262.

Two major policy reforms occurred in the 1980s to reduce Federal incentives to drain and clear wetlands: (1) the "swampbuster" provision of the Food Security Act of 1985, and (2) the Tax Reform Act of 1986. This article presents a stochastic simulation analysis of three representative counties in Louisiana, Arkansas, and Mississippi which shows that both reforms reduced the economic feasibility of wetland conversion.

176. **Kulshreshtha, S. N. and J. A. Gillies. 1993. "Economic Evaluation of Aesthetic Amenities: A Case Study of River View."** *Water Resources Bulletin* 29(2):257-266.

Presence of a river in an urban setting may contribute positively to an aesthetically pleasing environment. Such aesthetic effects are not typically linked to specific economic activities and occur, for example, when residents are exposed to a riverview. Qualities enhancing the aesthetic value of the river include the presence of parks, trails, and vegetation along the riverbanks. The value of aesthetic amenities provided by South Saskatchewan to the City of Saskatoon residents was estimated in this study using non-market methods. The implicit price of the river view was estimated using the Hedonic Price Model, whereas value through willingness-to-pay for property taxes or higher rents was also estimated using actual market data. The total annual value of the river to the City of Saskatoon through addition of aesthetic amenities was estimated at $1.2 million in 1989 dollars.

177. **Kusler, Jon A. and Sally Daly, eds. 1989.** *Wetlands and River Corridor Management: Proceedings of an International Symposium.* **Association of Wetland Managers, Inc., Omnipress, Madison, Wisconsin, 519 pp.**

Addresses river and stream corridor management, including adjacent riverine and estuarine wetlands, from the natural systems protection and restoration perspective. Includes chapters on aesthetic/recreational values and evaluation, modeling, and monitoring information systems. Includes entries 13, 58, 132, 147, 223, 224, and 412.

178. **Kusler, Jon A. and Richard Smardon, eds. 1990.** *Wetlands of the Great Lakes: Protection and Restoration Policies--Status of the Science.* **Proceedings of an International Symposium, Association of State Wetland Managers, Inc., Berne, New York, 335 pp.**

Papers focus upon government programs and policies for the protection and restoration of Great Lakes wetlands and the critical scientific issues in such protection and restoration. Papers make recommendations for strengthening protection and restoration efforts in light of what is known scientifically about the wetlands. Includes chapters on wetland education and aesthetics and wetland valuation. Includes entries 27, 98, 172, 253, and 269.

179. Langner, L. L. and R. E. Heimlich. 1989. "Economics of Wetland Preservation: The Agricultural Connection." Pp. 877-888 in *Freshwater Wetlands and Wildlife*, R. R. Sharitz and J. W. Gibbons, eds., Symposium Series No. 61, U.S. Department of Energy, Oak Ridge, Tennessee.
Data on nonfederal wetlands from the National Resources Inventory were used to analyze the potential for agricultural conversions, how potential conversions could impact critical wetland areas, and the effect of new agricultural policies on future conversions. Found that a majority of the nonfederal wetlands would be physically productive for agriculture, if converted. However, financial feasibility is limited, primarily by high conversion costs. Only 7 percent of the remaining nonfederal wetlands were rated as having a high or medium potential for conversion. The effectiveness of new farm legislation that denies farm program benefits to farmers cropping converted wetlands will depend on the level of farmer participation in these programs.

180. Lant, C. L. 1989. *Greenbelts: An Economic Analysis of Riparian Corridors in the Agricultural Midwest.* Thesis, University of Iowa, Iowa City, 276 pp.
Evaluates the effectiveness and economics of greenbelts and riparian wetland in Iowa and Illinois. Economic values are estimated for reductions in sediment concentrations using regression analysis. Contingent valuation estimates for improved river quality range from $35.50 to $47.16 per year per person.

181. Lant, Christopher L. 1991. "Potential of the Conservation Reserve Program to Control Agricultural Surface Water Pollution." *Environmental Management* 15(4):507-518.
Estimates potential enrollment of streamside and floodplain croplands in CRP program as a water quality improvement policy. Found through a contingent choice survey that enrollments in the program climb from less than 6 percent to over 83 percent as the annual rental rate is increased from $20 to $200 per acre. Also found that potential retirements decline

if tree planting, drainage removal, or a twenty year contract are required. Concludes that the potential of a CRP-based water-quality program to improve water quality is substantial but constrained by the economic trade-offs farmers make between crop production and conservation.

182. **Lant, Christopher and Steven E. Kraft. 1993.** *An Evaluation of Policy Tools to Establish Forests and Protect Water Quality in Cornbelt Watersheds.* **Water Resources Center, University of Illinois, Urbana, 20 pp.**
Utilizes two contingent valuation surveys on 770 mail samples and 157 personal interviews in ten cornbelt counties to estimate participation in the Conservation Reserve Program, Agricultural Wetland Reserve Program, and the Water Quality Incentives Program. Identifies possible barriers to increased enrollment and presents farmers' attitudes toward these programs as well as toward the Swampbuster provision. The most common reason (77.4 percent) for landowners to not enroll in the programs was economics. Respondents made their decisions based on the relative flows of income when not enrolled in the programs.

183. **Lant, C. L. and R. S. Roberts. 1990. "Greenbelts in the Cornbelts: Riparian Wetlands, Intrinsic Values, and Market Failure."** *Environment and Planning A* **22(10):1375-1388.**
Contrasts the economic value of riparian wetlands used for agricultural production with the value found through a contingent valuation survey. Concludes recreational values exceed agricultural values on a per acre basis in most instances. Suggests the Conservation Reserve Program expand to cover water quality, aquatic ecosystems, and intrinsic values.

184. **Leidy, Robert A., Peggy L. Fiedler, and Elisabeth R. Micheli. 1992. "Is Wetter Better?"** *Bio-Science* **42(1):58-62.**
Some environmental policymakers believe that the value of a given wetland environment is determined by how much water it contains. Studies of wetlands in arid regions indicate that the ecological gains from protecting less-wet wetlands are considerable.

185. **Leitch, Jay A. and Brenda L. Ekstrom. 1989.** *Wetland Economics and Assessment.* **Garland Publishing Inc., New York, 194 pp.**
Contains 561 mostly annotated entries in six areas: general; assessment; economic valuation; management; regulations, policies, and programs; and social values. Captures most of the wetland economics literature from 1975 to 1988, with more important works prior to 1975 included.

186. Leitch, Jay A. and James F. Baltezore. 1992. "The Status of North Dakota Wetlands." *Journal of Soil and Water Conservation* 47(3):216-219.
A case study of wetlands protection in Eddy County, North Dakota, was the basis for estimating that 35 percent of the state's wetlands, or about 700,000 acres, had a high degree of protection. Wetland protection legislation and incentive programs applicable to North Dakota are briefly reviewed. Property rights, attitudes, wetland definition, and how many wetlands are needed by society are identified as substantial unresolved issues. See also entry 92.

187. Lipske, Michael. 1990. "How Much Is Enough?" *National Wildlife* 28(4):16-23.
Discusses some of the potential effects of no-net-loss policies and the prospects of future development in Alaska's wetlands with particular reference to waterfowl.

188. Loomis, J., M. Hanemann, B. Kanninen, and T. Wegge. 1991. "Willingness to Pay to Protect Wetlands and Reduce Wildlife Contamination From Agricultural Drainage." Pp. 411-429 in *The Economics and Management of Water and Drainage in Agriculture,* A. Dinar and D. Zilberman, ed., Kluwer Academic Publishers, Dordrecht, The Netherlands.
Presents the results of a survey of the general population in California, regarding their willingness-to-pay for alternative programs to protect and expand wetlands, as well as to reduce wildlife contamination in the San Joaquin Valley. The results of 803 completed interviews from 1,573 successfully contacted households indicate that Californians would pay $154 each year in higher taxes to purchase water to prevent a decrease in wetland acreage from 85,000 acres to 27,000 acres. This value rose to $254 to provide for an increase in wetland acreage to 125,000 acres with an associated 40 percent increase of bird populations. California households would pay $313 each year in additional taxes to implement agricultural drainage programs that would reduce waterbird exposure to contamination from 70 percent to 20 percent exposure. The water management implication of these results is that Californians value clean water supplies for refuges at over $3 billion a year.

189. Loomis, John B., Thomas Wegge, Michael Hanemann, and Barbara Kannienen. 1990. "The Economic Value of Water to Wildlife and Fisheries in the San Joaquin Valley: Results of a Simulated Voter Referendum." Pp. 259-268 in *Transactions of the 55th North American Wildlife and Natural Resources Conference.*

Finds that the willingness-to-pay of Californians to reduce waterbird exposure to water contamination is $3 billion. Californians were also willing to pay $2.5 billion to increase the amount of wetlands in the state. Concludes that, given society's rising value for wildlife, far too little water has gone to wildlife and far too much to agriculture. Suggests modest reallocations, rather than wholesale changes, would make substantial improvements.

190.   Lovely, Jeffrey M. 1990. **"Protecting Wetlands: Consideration of Secondary Social and Economic Effects by the United States Army Corps of Engineers in its Wetlands Permitting Process."** *Boston College Environmental Affairs Law Review* **17(3):647-686.** Argues that the Corps should be granted broad discretion to protect wetlands as provided in Section 404. Contends that the Corps should not be limited in its consideration of wetland permits, as in Mall Properties, Inc. vs. Marsh, as secondary economic effects would go unassessed resulting in a bias toward the developer.

191.   Lugo, Ariel E. and Bruce Bayle. 1992. *Wetlands Management in the Caribbean and the Role of Forestry and Wetlands in the Economy: Proceedings of the Fifth Meeting of Caribbean Foresters at Trinidad.* **Southern Forest Experiment Station-Rio Piedras, Puerto Rico, Forest Service, U.S. Department of Agriculture, New Orleans, Louisiana, 115 pp.** Includes 17 papers from 12 different Caribbean nations covering management, regulations, and overviews.

192.   Luzar, E. Jane and Steven A. Henning, eds. 1989. *Alternative Perspectives on Wetland Evaluation and Use.* **SNREC Publication No. 27, Southern Rural Development Center, Mississippi State University, Mississippi State, 46 pp.** Proceedings of a regional workshop of the Southern Natural Resource Economics Committee in November 1988 at Baton Rouge Louisiana. Includes five papers, four of which are listed elsewhere. Includes entries 17, 43, 121, and 151.

193.   Ma, Xuehui, Xintu Liu, and Rongfen Wang. 1993. **"China's Wetlands and Agro-Ecological Engineering."** *Ecological Engineering* **2(3):291-301.** Provides an overview of China's wetlands and discusses how complex paddy-reed-fish wetland systems have brought about ecological and economic benefits in China. Quantifies rice, reed, and fish outputs.

194. Maddock, M. 1991. "Education, Research and Passive Recreation-
    An Integrated Program at the Wetlands Center, Shortland."
    International Journal of Science Education 13(5):561-568.
    Describes the Wetlands Center at Shortland, New South Wales, Australia
    which is a center for education, research and passive recreation in wetland
    settings.

195. Mercer, D. C. 1993. "Recreation and Wetlands: Impacts, Conflict,
    and Policy Issues." Pp. 267-295 in *Wetlands: A Threatened
    Landscape*, M. Williams, ed., Blackwell Publishers, Oxford,
    United Kingdom.
    Examines the relationships between wetlands and recreation and tourism.
    Presents case studies as examples from Amberley Wildbrooks, United
    Kingdom; Kakadn National Park, Northern Territory, Australia; and Dal
    Lake Kashmire, India.

196. Mermet, L. 1991. "Participation, Strategies and Ethics: Roles of
    People in Wetland Management." *Landscape Urban Ecology*
    20(1-3):231-237.
    Concentrates on a needed clarification of the concept of "managing"
    ecosystems. Generally, no one manager is in command of the evolution
    of a given wetland. On the other hand, management results from the
    activities and purposes of various actors with diverging intentions and
    unequal means. For progress to be made in the management of wetlands,
    a careful diagnosis of who is playing what part in the game and how, is
    a crucial element.

197. Mitchell, John G. 1992. "Our Disappearing Wetlands." *National
    Geographic* 182(4):3-45.
    Presents a layperson's overview discussion of the wetlands controversy
    in the United States.

198. Morris, J. 1989. "Land Drainage: Agricultural Benefits and
    Environmental Impacts." *Journal of the Institution of Water and
    Environmental Management* 3(6):551-557.
    Reviews the context and contribution of agricultural land drainage in the
    United Kingdom and discusses the design and performance of land drain-
    age improvement and maintenance schemes. The environmental impacts
    of land drainage are considered, and how drainage activities can be, and
    are being, modified to meet environmental criteria.

199. Moss, B. 1993. "Case Study: Lowland Wetland Conservation." Pp.
    136-149 in *Environmental Dilemmas: Ethics and Decisions*, R. J.

Berry, ed., Chapman and Hall Ltd., London, United Kingdom.
Explains the dilemma of wetland conservation and preservation; the conflict between immediate need and wise exploitation. Describes the nature of wetlands before looking at how they are used by humans. Discusses the vulnerability of wetlands as a fragile ecosystem.

200.   **Mukul. 1993. "Saving Calcutta Wetlands."** *Economic and Political Weekly* **28(49):2642.**
Discusses recent successes in saving Calcutta wetlands. Mentions some of the benefits of these wetlands such as waterfowl habitat and waste disposal.

201.   **Myhre, Mark A. 1992.** *Economic Analysis of Wetlands Drainage in Central Alberta.* **M.Sc. thesis, University of Alberta, Edmonton, Canada, 82 pp., (University Microfilms Inc., Order No: AADMM-77089).**
The economic feasibility of draining temporary wetlands in central Alberta is examined. Costs and benefits associated with two drainage systems are analyzed from the farmer's and from society's perspectives. On-site costs and benefits of the drainage system are included as well as wildlife habitat losses.

202.   **Nassar, J. Ron, Philip J. Zwank, David C. Hayden, and Jay V. Huner. 1991.** *Multiple-use Impoundments for Attracting Waterfowl and Producing Crawfish.* **Fish and Wildlife Service, U.S. Department of the Interior, National Wetlands Research Center, Slidell, Louisiana, 48 pp.**
Reviews waterfowl hunting, problems involved, crawfish farming, and increased interest in managing crawfish ponds for waterfowl. Also includes detailed information on constructing and managing multiple-use impoundments for attracting waterfowl and producing crawfish.

203.   **Ngoile, M. A. and J. P. Shunula. 1992. "Status and Exploitation of the Mangrove and Associated Fishery Resources in Zanzibar."** *Hydrobiologia* **247(1-3):229-234.**
Discusses the different types of fishery resources supported by mangrove swamps on Zanzibar Island. The mangroves also protect the coastline from erosion. Since the mangrove forests are being over exploited and subsequently fishery resources are declining, there is an urgent need for the introduction of effective management measures that would guarantee sustained utilization of the mangroves.

204. Nicholas, S. 1992. "The War Over Wetlands." *Issues in Science and Technology* 8(4):35-41.
Overview of the overall wetlands issue presented from a wetland protection proponent's perspective. Concludes that until a sound and persuasive model for calculating wetlands' true worth is devised, wetlands are likely to continue to disappear.

205. Okruszko, H. 1990. *Wetlands of the Biebrza Valley--Their Value and Future Management.* Section of Agriculture and Forestry, Polish Academy of Sciences, Warsaw, Poland, 107 pp.
Biebrza wetlands occupy a large depression in northeast Poland and cover an area of 116,000 ha. Their value results from the character and the uniqueness of its water and swamp ecosystems.

206. Organisation for Economic Co-operation and Development. 1992. *Market and Government Failures in Environmental Management: Wetlands and Forests.* Organisation for Economic Co-operation and Development, Paris, France, 82 pp.
Includes entry 72.

207. Palmer, James F. and Richard Smardon. 1988. "Human-Use Values of Wetlands: An Assessment in Juneau, Alaska." Pp. 108-114 in *Proceedings of the National Wetland Symposium: Urban Wetlands,* Jon A. Kusler, Sally Daly, and Gail Brooks, eds., Association of Wetland Managers, Inc., Berne, New York.
Develops a range of criteria to evaluate human-use values for wetlands in Juneau, Alaska. Established a ranking of wetland activities based on the percent of residents participating. Included in entry 48.

208. Pannier, Federico and Rosario Fraino de Pannier. 1989. *Mangrove Swamps of Venezuela.* Manglares de Venezuela, Lagoven, Caracas, Venezuela, 67 p.

209. Peltzer, R. H. M. 1989. "The Impact of Recreation on Nature in The Netherlands." Pp. 125-149 in *Leisure and the Environment: Proceedings,* B. J. H. Brown, ed., Leisure Studies Association, Bournemouth, United Kingdom.

210. Phillips, W. E., T. J. Haney, and W. L. Adamowicz. 1993. "An Economic Analysis of Wildlife Habitat Preservation in Alberta." Paper presented at the Symposium on *Economics of Wetlands*

Preservation on Agricultural Land in Western Canada, **Western Agricultural Economics Association and the Canadian Agricultural Economics and Farm Management Society, Edmonton, Alberta, Canada.**
Focuses on wildlife habitat quality change and its perception by humans. First, from the user perspective based on measures of willingness-to-pay benefits using a discrete choice contingent valuation method; and secondly, from a private landowner perspective who provides some of the habitat that benefits users, using a multi-nominal logit technique. Habitat quality change scenarios were used to determine benefits to determine landowner attitudes towards habitat retention and enhancement options.

211. **Porter, Richard M. and G. Cornelis van Kooten. 1993.** *Wetlands Preservation on the Canadian Prairies: The Problem of the Public Duck.* **Department of Agricultural Economics and Department of Forest Resources Management, University of British Columbia, Vancouver, Canada, 21 pp.**
Provides background material and presents a brief overview of a southeastern Saskatchewan wetland preservation project which is part of a larger study of habitat protection programs established in the Canadian prairie provinces. The intent of the project was to determine the value of wetlands in terms of waterfowl so an appropriate subsidy could be formulated to encourage farmers to retain wetlands.

212. **Post, Roger A. 1990.** *Effects of Petroleum Operations in Alaskan Wetlands: A Critique.* **Technical Report No. 90-3, Habitat Division, Alaska Department of Fish and Game, Juneau, 112 pp.**
A point-by-point critique of Senner (1989) (entry 222), who presents the petroleum industry's perspective. Argues that Senner's report does not accurately portray the ecological and socioeconomic values of arctic-tundra wetlands. Concludes (1) tundra wetlands are not that different from other wetlands, (2) habitat controls arctic wildlife species, (3) wildlife population monitoring is not the way to manage wetlands, and (4) habitat protection is cost-effective for fish and wildlife.

213. **Pringle, C., G. Vellidis, F. Heliotis, D. Bandacu, and S. Cristofor. 1993.** **"Environmental Problems of the Danube Delta."** *American Scientist* **81(4):350-361.**
Catalogs the many environmental problems in the Danube River Delta. Discusses some of the losses of economic resources such as shellfish and fishery. Outlines recent World Bank efforts to reverse the decline in these resources and develop environmentally sustainable activities.

214. **Richards, S. F. and E. P. Flint. 1990. "Long-Term Transformations in the Sundarbans Wetlands Forest of Bengal."** *Agriculture and Human Values* **7(2):17-33.**
The landscape of the Sundarbans of Bengal is a product of two countervailing forces: conversion of wetland mangrove forests to cropland and preservation of the forests in reserves to be managed for long-term sustained yield of wood products. In the late nineteenth century, as the rate of agricultural conversion increased, the colonial Forest Department successfully sought to preserve large areas of the remaining Sundarbans tidal forest by giving them the legal status of Reserved or Protected Forests. Concludes that despite the burgeoning population of India and Bangladesh, expansion of cropland has taken place outside the Sundarbans. Overexploitation of these forests remains a possibility, but large scale clearing for rice paddies is unlikely under present government policies which favor the forests as preservations.

215. **Richardson, J. L. and J. L. Arndt. 1989. "What Use Prairie Potholes?"** *Journal of Soil and Water Conservation* **44(3):196-198.**
Stresses the hydrologic and soil factors for determining uses of wetlands in the prairie pothole region. Discusses the uses of two different types of wetlands: (1) ephemeral or seasonal wetlands provide important wildlife habitat but also have the best soil characteristics for agriculture, and (2) semipermanent ponds or water flow-through wetlands provide important habitat for wildlife. Salinity is also discussed.

216. **Rogers, F. E. J., K. H. Rogers, and J. S. Buzer. 1985.** *Wetlands for Wastewater Treatment.* **Witwatersrand University Press, Johannesburg, South Africa, 122 pp.**
Assesses the use of natural and manipulated wetlands for wastewater treatment in South Africa. Concludes that (1) wetlands are effective in reducing some elements, but not others; (2) the use of wetlands for wastewater treatment appears to be both feasible and economically beneficial; and (3) little is known about the effects of wastewater application on wetland ecosystems.

217. **Rubin, Debra K. 1993. "Protections Sink Value."** *Environment and Natural Resources* **230(23):7-9.**
The New Jersey Superior Court upheld a ruling that dramatically cut the tax assessment on the Berry's Creek property in the state's Meadowland region. Tougher environmental legislation has meant that the property is now unlikely to get development approval, thus cutting its assessed value.

218. Salvesen, David. 1990. *Wetlands: Mitigating and Regulating Development Impacts.* The Urban Land Institute, Washington, D.C., 115 pp.
Discusses history and the present course of wetlands with particular reference to human intervention. Includes individually referenced chapters on the nature of wetlands, federal wetlands regulation, and mitigation strategies.

219. Saskatchewan Wetland Conservation. 1993. "The Economics of Converting Wetlands to Croplands." *Farm Management Facts,* Water Series No. 1, Saskatoon, 12 pp.
Provides worksheet-type analysis to estimate the profitability of prairie wetland conversions.

220. Scoones, I., ed. 1991. "Overview--Ecological, Economics, and Social Issues." Part 1 in *Wetlands in Drylands: The Agroecology of Savanna Systems in Africa,* International Institute for Environment and Development, London, 82 pp.
Explores the nature and use of variability in the agricultural and pastoral landscapes of dryland Africa. The importance of these areas is explained by considering the dynamics of the farming and pastoral systems in terms of seasonal and interannual changes, biophysical properties of the resource and historical changes as pressures increase or recede.

221. Scoones, I. 1992. *Wetlands in Drylands: Key Resources for Agricultural and Pastoral Production in Africa.* Issues Paper No. 38, Drylands Programme, International Institute for Environment and Development, London, 23 pp.

222. Senner, Robert G. B. 1989. *Effects of Petroleum Operations in Alaskan Wetlands.* Robert Senner and Company for ARCO Alaska, Inc. and BP Exploration (Alaska) Inc., Anchorage, Alaska, 138 pp.
Discusses the effect of petroleum operations on Alaskan wetlands, with emphasis on arctic tundra wetlands of the North Slope. Compares the values of Alaskan wetlands with those of wetlands in the lower 48 states. Concludes that (1) North Slope wetlands do not provide most of the values associated with wetlands in the lower 48, (2) cumulative wetland losses in Alaska are extremely low, (3) North Slope mitigation approaches currently in effect are successful, and (4) North Slope wetland policy should be different than for wetlands in the lower 48 states. See also entry 212.

223. **Smardon, Richard C. 1989. "Documenting View-scapes of the St. Lawrence River." Pp. 178-191 in** *Wetlands and River Corridor Management: Proceedings of an International Symposium,* **Jon A. Kusler and Sally Daly, eds., Association of Wetland Managers, Inc., Omnipress, Madison, Wisconsin.**
Reports on the methods and results of a study which produced a ranking of positive and negative landscape attributes for land along the St. Lawrence River. Included in entry 177.

224. **Smardon, Richard C. 1989. "Management to Protect River Corridor Wetland Scenic Values." Pp. 168-171 in** *Wetlands and River Corridor Management: Proceedings of an International Symposium,* **Jon A. Kusler and Sally Daly, eds., Association of Wetland Managers, Inc., Omnipress, Madison, Wisconsin.**
Briefly discusses river corridor recreation activities, documenting river corridor aesthetic resources relevant to these activities, assessing aesthetic resources, and managing river corridors to protect these resources. Included in entry 177.

225. **Smit, H. and H. Coops. 1991. "Ecological, Economic and Social Aspects of Natural and Man-made Bulrush** *Scirpus lacustris L.* **Wetlands in The Netherlands."** *Landscape Urban Ecology* **20(1-3):33-40.**
The historical and present day occurrence of bulrush *Scirpus lacustris L.* is closely related to human use. During the last few decades bulrush stands declined in the two main growing areas in The Netherlands. Factors that contributed to the decline are evaluated. Bulrush growing is still profitable, providing perspectives for a beneficial wetland management. Exploitation of natural and artificial bulrush stands can contribute to a sustainable and wise wetland use.

226. **Smith, V. Kerry. 1992. "Environmental Costing for Agriculture: Will it be Standard Fare in the Farm Bill of 2000?"** *American Journal of Agricultural Economics* **74(5):1076-1088.**
Discusses the environmental costs associated with agricultural activities. Uses wetlands conversion as an example of an environmental cost. Outlines some conceptual foundations for environmental costing in terms of its measurement and attributing environmental externalities. Concludes that without adequate research, policies introducing environmental costs as part of the social costs of different agricultural activities may not move us any closer to using marketed and nonmarketed environmental resources efficiently.

227. **Somowitz, Samuel. 1993. "Cut Owners' Tax Bills Down to Size."** *Real Estate Today* **26:46-49.**
Outlines information on assessment of wetlands as it relats to tax valuation of residential real estate.

228. **Soutiere, Edward C. 1990. "Waterfowl: Income Potential and Problems."** Pp. 147-157 in *Income Opportunities for the Private Landowner Through Management of Natural Resources and Recreational Access,* **William N. Grafton, Anthony Ferrise, Dale Colyer, Dennis K. Smith, and James E. Miller, eds., R.D. No. 740, West Virginia University Extension Sevice, Morgantown.**
Discusses waterfowl hunting as a way wetland owners can capture some of the benefits of wetlands and lead to improved habitat. Hunters are willing to pay from $7 to $250 per day to hunt waterfowl. Provides examples of fees charged from 20 eastern U.S. locations. Included in item 142.

* **Stavins, Robert N. 1990. "Alternative Renewable Resource Strategies: A Simulation of Optimal Use."**
Cited above as entry 66.

229. **Stavins, Robert N. and Adam B. Jaffe. 1990. "Unintended Impacts of Public Investments on Private Decisions: The Depletion of Forested Wetlands."** *American Economic Review* **80(3):337-352.**
Demonstrates that the depletion of forested wetlands in the Mississippi Valley has been, and is currently, exacerbated by federal policy to protect wetlands. Utilizes a model to aggregate individual land use decisions using a parametric distribution of unobserved land quality. The model quantifies the impact of federal projects and other factors on wetlands.

230. **Steinberg, Robert E. 1991.** *Wetlands and Real Estate Development Handbook.* **2nd edition, Government Institutes, Inc., Rockville, Maryland, 218 pp.**

231. **Steinhart, Peter. 1990. "No Net Loss: As Wetlands Vanish, We Begin to Recognize Their Value."** *Audubon* **92(4):18-22.**
Begins with a case involving disagreement over whether or not 156 acres on the edge of San Francisco Bay is or is not wetland. Discusses the history of wetland legislation in the U.S. Concludes with a brief look at the role of wetland in Western culture.

232. **Stockdale, Erik. 1992.** *Freshwater Wetlands, Urban Stormwater, and Nonpoint Pollution Control: A Literature Review and Annotated*

Bibliography. **Environmental Division, King County Resource Planning, Bellevue, Washington, 267 pp.**
Provides information on the wetland permit process with regard to the regulations, the process, the role of the Federal Government and its agencies' applicable laws, challenging decisions, wetland real estate transactions, and enforcement actions.

233. **Stokoe, Peter, Jane Roots, and Brad Walters. 1989.** *Application of Wetland Evaluation Methodologies to the Minudie Dykelands, Nova Scotia.* **Report 5 of** *Wetlands are not Wastelands*, **Sustainable Development Branch, Canadian Wildlife Service and Wildlife Habitat Canada, Ottawa, 88 pp.**
As with the three other studies (items 20, 94, 138) in the "Wetlands are not Wastelands" project, this study sought to estimate the societal value of the relevant wetlands by using a willingness-to-pay approach, opportunity cost method, and cumulative impact approach. Found the willingness-to-pay approach results were severely hampered by starting point biases, as the Dykelands are currently utilized for agricultural production. In the opportunity cost method, rough calculation showed that the new benefit for each differential use of tidal land show small quantified net benefits on the order of tens, or at most hundreds of dollars per hectare year, as well as additional unquantified benefits, from freshwater marsh. The cumulative impact approach found the establishment of waterfowl habitat to be the most compelling. (See entry 8).

234. **Stone, J. A. and D. E. Legg. 1992.** "Agriculture and the Everglades." *Journal of Soil and Water Conservation* **47(3):207-215.**
Provides an overview of the current controversy over land use in the Everglades in light of the lawsuit filed by the Federal Government against the South Florida Water Management District (SFWMD) and the Florida Department of Environmental Regulation. The suit claimed that the agencies had failed to regulate polluted water flowing into Everglades land owned by the Federal Government. Discusses historical drainage of the Everglades, agricultural practices, water management, and the Recommended Best Management Practices for reducing the overall agricultural impact. The SFWMD Everglades Surface Water Improvement and Management projects, including construction of the stormwater treatment areas, are estimated to cost $319 million. Costs of implementing BMPs are expected to initially reach $62 per acre for producers, then $3 to $4 for subsequent annual costs.

235. **Stutz, Bruce. 1992.** "Not in Whose Backyard?" *Audubon* **94(5):120.**
Environmental protection regulations are conveniently exploited as a

collective excuse to hinder the construction of affordable housing. The Department of Housing and Urban Development is contributing to this myth because it measures economic growth only in terms of new housing starts and restoration of existing housing.

236. **Thomas, C. H. 1987. "Preserving Environmental Values." Pp. 52-61 in *Farm Drainage in the United States: History, Status, and Prospects*, George A Pavelis, ed., Miscellaneous Publication 1455, U.S. Department of Agriculture, Washington, D.C.**
Argues that drainage assessments are incomplete without considering environmental impacts. Discusses wetland functions and ecological concerns in the context of agricultural production. Concludes food and fiber production should be balanced with the other products of land, including those produced by wetlands.

237. **Thomas, David H. L., Fethi Ayache, and G. Edward Hollis. 1991. "Use and Non-Use Values in the Conservation of Ichkeul National Park, Tunisia." *Environmental Conservation* 18(2):119-130.**
The establishment of the Ichkeul National Park in northern Tunisia was based primarily on non-use, existence values, but the survival of its wetlands is now threatened by dam construction. The economic gains from taking measures to prevent degradation of the wetlands, namely by releases of water from the dams to maintain the marshes, would outweigh the economic benefits from the use of water in agricultural irrigation, and effectively maintain much of the international significance of the National Park and its surroundings.

238. **Thompson, John and Don A. Young. 1992. "The Optimal Use of Prairie Pothole Wetlands: An Economic Perspective." *Canadian Water Resources Journal* 17(4):365-372.**
Uses the methods described in the "Wetlands are not Wastelands" project (entry 8) to compare the recreational benefits of two study wetlands against their value if converted into agricultural land for typical farms in the King George and Lost River Area in Saskatchewan. Average annual benefit per hectare for recreational uses is estimated at $105. Converting these particular wetlands to agricultural land would impose a cost of $29 to $70 per hectare annually.

239. **Times Mirror Magazines Conservation Council. 1992. "Natural Resources: Can They be Saved?" *Field and Stream* 97(3):28-30.**
A survey reveals that 92 percent of Americans desire a balance between environmental protection and economic growth. The public needs to be

educated as to the importance of wetlands, and many are content with the
amount of natural lands open to the public.

240. **Tuohy, W. 1993. "Characterizing the San Francisco Estuary: A
Case Study of Science Management in the National Estuary
Program."** *Coastal Management* **21:113-129.**

241. **Tuohy, William S. 1994. "Neglect of Market Incentives in Local
Environmental Planning: A Case Study."** *Coastal Management*
22:81-95.
This analysis of the San Francisco Estuary Project's decision-making links
inaction regarding market incentives in its environmental management
plan to lack of relevant expertise, attitudes among constituencies, project
management, and inattention to details of implementation. Questions are
raised about the ability of local policy leaders to formulate and implement
market incentives.

242. **Turner, R. K. and R. J. Brooke. 1988. "Management and Valuation
of an Environmentally Sensitive Area: Norfolk Broadland,
England, Case Study."** *Environmental Management* **12(2):
193-207.**
Assesses the various techniques available for evaluating the wetland
resource in the development versus conservation conflict situation. The
search for an acceptable flood alleviation strategy for the environmental
asset structure of the study is examined at two levels. A basic screening
system is applied to each of the identified flood protection planning units
to enable the rank ordering of the units. A more detailed appraisal is then
made of the value of selected units so that cost-effectiveness can be
assessed. Specific management issues and their likely effect on the
environment are also addressed.

243. **Turner, R. Kerry and Tom Jones, eds. 1991.** *Wetlands: Market and
Intervention Failures, Four Case Studies.* **Earthscan Publications
Limited, London, 192 pp.**
Presents four case studies commissioned by the organization of Economic
Cooperation and Development (OECD) respectively from the United
States, the United Kingdom, France, and Spain.

* **Turner, R. Kerry. 1993.** *Sustainable Environmental Economics and
Management: Principles and Practice.*
Cited above as entry 73.

244. **U.S. Congress, Committee on Small Business. 1991.** *Effects of Wetlands Protection Regulations on Small Business.* **102nd Congress, 1st Session, Hearings before the Committee on Small Business, House of Representatives, U.S. Government Printing Office, Washington, D.C., vi, 1426 p.: illustrations and maps.**

245. **U.S. Department of the Interior. 1988.** *The Impact of Federal Programs on Wetlands. Volume I: The Lower Mississippi Alluvial Plain and the Prairie Pothole Region.* **Office of the Secretary, Washington, D.C., 114 pp.**
The first of two reports to Congress, this volume covers the Lower Mississippi Alluvial Plain and the Prairie Pothole Region. Volume II (forthcoming) covers all other major wetland regions in the U.S. Conclusions for the Delta region include (1) federal projects accounted for about 25 percent of total wetland depletion between 1935 and 1984; (2) while historically profitable, wetland conversion for agricultural production opportunities are limited; (3) agricultural supports and tax treatment increased the profitability of wetland conversion; and (4) Delta wetlands remain vulnerable to conversion in the long run. Conclusions regarding prairie potholes include (1) federal agriculture programs significantly increased the profitability of drainage, (2) tax incentives have not been a strong incentive to drain, (3) roadway construction has facilitated drainage, (4) government water management programs have affected many wetlands, and (5) most unprotected wetlands are subject to eventual drainage.

246. **U.S. Department of the Interior. 1988.** *Concept Plan for Waterfowl Habitat Protection: Prairie Potholes and Parklands.* **Region 3, Fish and Wildlife Service, Minneapolis, Minnesota, 21 pp.**
Discusses the goals, objectives, and strategies for production of prime waterfowl breeding habitat in the Prairie Pothole Region. Lists the accomplishments and objectives of the waterfowl habitat acquisition programs in the region. Outlines the strategies for further habitat protection.

247. **U.S. Department of the Interior. 1989.** *National Wetlands Priority Conservation Plan.* **Fish and Wildlife Service, Washington, D.C., 58 pp.**
The National Wetlands Priority Conservation plan provides a planning framework, criteria, and guidance intended to meet the requirements of section 301 of the Emergency Wetlands Resources Act. Criteria to be

considered in determining acquisition priorities include functions and values of wetlands, historic wetland losses, and threat for future wetland losses.

248. **U.S. Department of the Interior. 1993.** *Wetlands of International Importance.* **Fish and Wildlife Service, Washington, D.C., 11 pp.**
Discusses the United States' participation in the "Ramsar" Convention (the Convention on Wetlands of International Importance Especially as Waterfowl Habitat). Also mentions objectives, obligations, areas covered, and operations of the convention. Wetlands values included economic benefits, biological diversity, and vital habitat.

249. **van Kooten, G. Cornelis. 1993. "Bioeconomic Evaluation of Government Agricultural Programs on Wetlands Conversion."** *Land Economics* **69(1):27-38.**
An evaluation of government agricultural support programs in terms of their net effect on wetlands conversions in Canada. The North American Waterfowl Management Plan was initiated in 1986 to preserve wetland areas as waterfowl habitats by paying farmers $30 per acre of unconverted land. In contrast, grain support programs pay $50-$60 per acre, resulting in the conversion of 81 percent of the total wetlands of the area to agricultural use. Without such subsidies, some 43 percent of the area will remain untouched as waterfowl habitats.

250. **van Kooten, G. C. 1993.** *Land Resource Economics and Sustainable Development: Economic Policies and the Common Good.* **University of British Columbia Press, Vancouver, Canada, 450 pp.**
A comprehensive introduction to land use and the economic tools to assess and resolve land use conflicts. A section on the role of government includes preservation of wildland and wetland preservation policies.

251. **van Kooten, G. C. and A. Schmitz. 1992. "Preserving Waterfowl Habitat on the Canadian Prairies: Economic Incentives Versus Moral Suasion."** *American Journal of Agricultural Economics* **74(1):79-89.**
Examines a pilot project of North American Waterfowl Management Plan (NAWMP) that encourages farmers to promote or maintain waterfowl habitat by relying not only on economic incentives but on awareness, education, and moral suasion. The pilot project relies on farmers' attitudes to keep payments low because project payments substitute for

grain program subsidies, thus constituting a transfer from Canadian taxpayers to U.S. contributors to NAWMP. A survey instrument and regression analysis are used to examine attitudes, economic incentives, willingness-to-pay, and willingness-to-accept compensation for modifying land use in order to conserve waterfowl habitat. The results indicate that current economic incentives offered to agricultural producers are inadequate because they ignore non-market costs, and that a positive attitude toward habitat preservation cannot be used as a substitute for monetary incentives.

252. van Vuuren, Willem and Pierre Roy. 1989. "Economic Evaluation of Wetland Preservation." Pp. 229-234 in *Wetlands: Inertia or Momentum*, Michal J. Bardecki and Nancy Patterson, eds., Federation of Ontario Naturalists, Don Mills, Ontario, Canada.
A case study of marshes around Lake St. Clair, Ontario, estimates dollar values for the social and private net benefits from both preservation and agriculture of various sizes and types of wetlands. Included in entry 14.

253. van Vuuren, Willem and Pierre Roy. 1990. "Determining Compensation Payments for Wetland Preservation." In *Wetlands of the Great Lakes: Protection and Restoration Policies--Status of the Science*, Jon A. Kusler and Richard Smardon, eds., Proceedings of an International Symposium, Association of State Wetland Managers, Inc., Berne, New York.
Through two cost-benefit analyses--from the perspective of the owner and that of society--it is ascertained whether or not preservation benefits outweigh benefits from conversion for society as a whole. The minimum purchase price for a wetland was found to be $4120/ha and the minimum conservation easement to preserve a wetland to be $2123/ha. Included in entry 178.

254. van Vuuren, Willem and Pierre Roy. 1990. "The Returns from Wetland Preservation Versus Reclamation for Agriculture." Meeting abstract, *Canadian Journal of Agricultural Economics-Revue Canadienne D'economie Rurale* 38(4):1028.
Briefly discusses differences in private and social returns for the St. Clair marshes in southwestern Ontario.

255. van Vuuren, Willem and Pierre Roy. 1990. "Social and Private Returns from Wetland Preservation." Pp. 553-563 in *International and Trans-boundary Water Resources Issues*, American Water Resources Association, Bethesda, Maryland.
See the following entry 256.

256. van Vuuren, Willem and Pierre Roy. 1993. "The Private and Social Returns from Wetland Preservation Versus Those From Wetland Conversion to Agriculture." *Ecological Economics* 8(3):289-305.

Compares the social net benefits of preservation to the private net benefits from conversion to agriculture in a case study of Lake St. Clair, Ontario. Social net benefits from preservation were found to exceed those from conversion, while private net benefits from conversion to agriculture exceeded those from preservation. This difference between private and social net benefits is due to drainage subsidies and property taxes, inability of wetland owners to extract payment for all preservation benefits originating from their wetland but occurring outside their boundaries, and inability of owners to extract consumers' surplus created on such land.

257. Verheugt, W. J. M., A. Purwoko, F. Danielsen, H. Skov, R. Kadaris-man, and R. Haskoning. 1991. "Integrating Mangrove and Swamp Forests Conservation with Coastal Lowland Development: The Banyuasin Sembilang Swamps Case Study, South Sumatra Province, Indonesia." *Landscape Urban Ecology* 20(1-3):85-94.

Describes the biological importance of the Banyuasin Sembilang Delta, indicating the current patterns of resource use by the local communities and their socioeconomic values (such as a fishery resource). It reviews the existing and scheduled large-scale development projects for, and adjacent to, the delta. An integrated land use/conservation plan for the Banyuasin Sembilang Delta is proposed, which accommodates the need for future small-scale swamp land development with conservation of the fragile but rich biological resources.

258. Wade, Max. 1990. "Ditches and Drains: The Ecology and Conservation of an Important Wetland Refuge." Pp. 77-93 in *Water, Engineering, and Landscape: Water Control and Landscape Transformation in the Modern Period*, Denis Cosgrove and Geoff Petts, eds., Belhaven Press, New York.

Suggests drainage channels make important contributions to wildlife habitat and the landscape ecology of the U.K.'s fenlands. Concludes there is an increasing need for integrated land use management strategies for these polder areas.

259. Walbridge, Mark R. 1993. "Functions and Values of Forested Wetlands in the Southern United States." *Journal of Forestry* 91(5):15-19.

Identifies some specific functions and values of palustrine forested wetlands. Focuses on the biogeochemical functions of wetlands which provide improved water quality and suggests strategies for wise use and management.

260. **Walter, John. 1989. "Farming in the Flyways."** *Successful Farming* **87(6):59-61.**
Briefly describes an incentive program to recognize farmers for conserving wetlands in the northern prairies. An example of positive publicity about wetlands in the popular agricultural press.

261. **Walter, John. 1990. "Some Farmers Even Believe that Wetlands Can Make a Farm More Valuable."** *Successful Farming* **88(8):73.**
An example of wetlands economics in the popular media. Identifies the difference between ecological and market values of wetlands.

262. **Want, William L. 1989.** *Law of Wetlands Regulation.* **Clark Boardman Callaghan, Deerfield, Illinois, 1 vol., (various pagings).**

263. **"Wetlands: Critical Links in Natural Ecosystems." 1990.** *Popular Science* **237(4):9.**
Follows statement by President George Bush (entry 108). Outlines past and current wetland issues and legislation.

264. **Whitehead, John C. 1990. "Measuring Willingness-to-pay for Wetlands Preservation with the Contingent Valuation Method."** *Wetlands* **10(2): 187-201.**
Presented a dichotomous choice to Kentucky households between the preservation of Clear Creek wetland, Kentucky and surface coal mining. Coefficients of the logistic regression generate estimates of mean willingness-to-pay in the range of $6 and $13 for each Kentucky household for preservation of 5,000 acres (13,000 km^2) of the Clear Creek wetland.

265. **Whitehead, J. C. 1991. "Measuring Contingent Values for Wetlands: Effect of Information About Related Environmental Goods."** *Water Resources Research* **27(10):2523-2531.**
Estimates willingness-to-pay for preservation of the Clear Creek wetland in western Kentucky when faced with surface coal mine lake reclamation and, in the initial independent format, increases of information about a nearby, publicly owned, wetland area. These findings suggest that the lack of explicit information about related environmental goods in contingent markets can contribute to a misstatement of willingness-to-pay.

* **Whitehead, J. C. 1992. "Measuring Use Value From Recreation Participation."**
  Cited above as entry 78.

266. **Whitehead, J. C. 1993. "Economic Valuation of Wetland Resources: A Review of the Value Estimates."** *Journal of Environmental Systems* **22(2):151-161.**
   Following the recognition that wetlands are valuable ecosystems and the necessary methodological developments, economists have attempted to estimate monetary values for wetland resources. Estimated economic values for wetland resources have been significantly greater than zero. However, several studies that estimate wetland values consider only a subset of wetland functions and services and, therefore, only partially measure the total value of wetland resources to society. Other studies may overestimate wetland values due to double-counting of value components. Discusses net factor income method, contingent valuation method, travel cost method, hedonic price method, and damage cost method.

267. **Whitehead, John C. and Peter A. Groothuis. 1992. "Economic Benefits of Improved Water Quality: A Case Study of North Carolina's Tar-Pamlico River."** *Rivers* **3(3):170-178.**
   Benefits of best management practices to reduce agricultural nonpoint source pollution were assessed using the contingent valuation method. Concludes that respondents are willing to pay for improved water quality. Aggregate benefits of improved water quality would be $1.62 million each year. A majority of voters would approve a program that would raise up to $1.06 million per year.

268. **Whitehead, J. C. and C. Y. Thompson. 1993. "Environmental Preservation Demand: Altruistic, Bequest, and Intrinsic Motives."** *American Journal of Economics and Sociology* **51(1): 19-30.**
   Demonstrates the importance of motivating attitudes on environmental preservation demand. The existing definitions of motives for preservation demand are set forth, then in an empirical case study, the contingent valuation method is used to reveal the behavioral intentions toward the preservation demand for wetlands in Kentucky. Motives for environmental preservation, attitudes towards development, and financial responsibility are included in a discrete choice model of preservation demand. It is shown that individuals have demand for preservation even though they have never visited or participated in on-site use of wetlands. Motives and attitudes are believed to play an important explanatory role in the demand for wetlands preservation.

269. Whittam, Bob. 1990. "Wetland Protection Through Local Economic Benefits and Public Education." In *Wetlands of the Great Lakes: Protection and Restoration Policies--Status of the Science*, Jon A. Kusler and Richard Smardon, eds., Proceedings of an International Symposium, Association of State Wetland Managers, Inc., Berne, New York, 335 pp.
Describes recent activities of Friends of Wye Marsh, Inc. Midland, Ontario. Focuses on the potential for conserving wetlands through *in situ* public education programs. Included in entry 178.

270. Williams, M. 1991. "The Human Use of Wetlands." *Progress in Human Geography* 15:1-22.
Attempts to explain and trace the main trends in the changing human attitudes and perceptions of wetlands in light of the paradox between "pride in achievement," and "concern at loss." Includes sections on the archaeology of wetlands, agricultural impacts, urban and industrial impacts, and recreational impacts.

271. Willingham, Phillip W. 1989. "Wetlands Harvesting Scott Paper Company." Pp. 63-66 in *Proceedings: Symposium on the Forested Wetlands of the Southern United States*, Donal D. Hook and Russ Lea, eds., Southeastern Forest Experiment Station, Forest Service, U.S. Department of Agriculture, Asheville, North Carolina.
Wetlands in the Mobile-Tensaw River Delta have been logged for Cypress and Tupelo Gum since the early 1700's using various systems consistent with the technology of the times. In 1984, Scott Paper Company began experimenting with cable logging designs to determine the most economical and least site damaging method but found cable systems generally unsatisfactory. In 1986, helicopter logging was tested and determined to be cost effective, safe, and least damaging to wetland sites. This paper describes experiences and results using both systems and other ongoing research for better wetlands logging systems. Included in entry 41.

272. Woodfall, David. 1989. "The Inexorable Marsh of Development." *World Magazine* 31(Nov.):36-41.

273. Young, Don A. 1989. *Toward Conservation/Management of Saskatchewan's Soil and Water Resources*. Environmental Management Associates (Saskatchewan) Ltd., Regina, Saskatchewan, Canada, 94 pp.

Intends to stimulate discussion among governmental and non-governmental organizations and to act as a catalyst in the process of land use planning which will lead to solutions for soil and water resources and to a strategy for sustained economic development.

274. **Young, Don A. 1990.** *Prairie Pothole Wetlands: Functions and Values.* **Report 7 of** *Wetlands are not Wastelands,* **Sustainable Development Branch, Canadian Wildlife Service and Wildlife Habitat Canada, Ottawa, 88 pp.**
Found two forms of benefits result from wetland drainage. First, drained land can be cultivated. The net value of production was found to be about $65 to $111 per hectare. Second, elimination of wetlands can lead to increased farming efficiency on adjacent lands and these benefits were determined to typically range from $58 to $77 per hectare of wetland drained. Typical wetland drainage and land preparation costs were found to be about $1,605 per hectare. Determined, using these costs, that additional drainage of wetlands on a typical 1.5 section farm was not economical. Found recreational benefits from a Saskatchewan perspective to range between $68 to $163 per hectare. From a continental perspective, where U.S. benefits for waterfowl are included, the study area wetlands ranged from $156 to $249 per hectare. See also entry 8.

275. **Zimmerer, Karl S. 1991. "Wetland Production and Smallholder Persistence: Agricultural Change in a Highland Peruvian Region."** *The Annals of the Association of American Geographers* **81(3): 443-463.**
Integrates regional political ecology concepts via the ideas of structuration, a politics of place, and production ecology in order to examine the ecological and social relations embodied in wetland agriculture. Montane bogs were converted into fields roughly 20 years ago when peasant cultivators in Colquepata District (southern Peru) responded to a convergence of production and demand incentives. Environmental conditions, regional social and economic structures, and government policy most shaped the temporal and spatial realization of these stimuli. Both the expansion of local commerce and the capture of state agricultural subsidies depended on social relations that formed historically through ethnic and peasant resistance against landlord domination in a "region of resistance." Flexible labor allocation required by the biological ecology of wetland fields has contributed to the persistence of production by peasant smallholders. The social practices and struggles of dominated peasants, as well as the ecology of production, etch critical temporal and spatial dimensions in the processes of agricultural change, capitalist development, and associated environmental transformations.

WETLAND RESTORATION/ CREATION ECONOMICS

OVERVIEW

Wetlands are being restored for a variety of beneficial and also bureaucratic reasons. However, little is known about the ecological successes of restoration, much less the economic efficiency of the investments. Abundant literature exists on the concepts of restoration or creation, but scant sources are available on economic costs and benefits with the exception of some recent work by King and Costanza (1994). For the 21st time, the annual conference on wetlands restoration and creation was held in Tampa, Florida in the spring of 1994, however almost all the presentations over the years have been "how to"; few have been concerned with economics.

This section contains manuscripts spanning a broad range of restoration and creation literature, hopefully capturing the majority of those where economics is an explicit component. With more and more emphasis on restoration and creation, it becomes even more important that economic analyses be carried out.

REFERENCE

King, Dennis and Robert Costanza. 1994. *The Cost of Wetland Creation and Restoration*. University of Maryland Center for Environmental and Estuarine Studies, for U.S. Department of Energy, Pittsburgh Energy Tech. Center, Pittsburgh, Pennsylvania.

SELECTED BIBLIOGRAPHY

276. Aadland, Hope. 1993. "Partners for Wildlife: A Win-Win Situation." *North Dakota Water* 1(2):15-18.
Explains how ranchers find value in keeping wetlands on agricultural land through implementation of the U.S. Fish and Wildlife Service Partners for Wildlife Program, which began in 1987. Over 255 landowners have created 1,011 acres of wetland habitat for a total cost of $243,500. The average size of wetland is 4 acres with an average creation cost of $240/acre.

277. Aadland, Hope. 1994. "Partners for Wildlife." *North Dakota Water* 2(2):27-30.
Nearly 15,000 acres of wetland had been restored in North Dakota by the end of 1993 through the U.S. Fish and Wildlife Service Partners for Wildlife Program. A followup on entry 276.

278. Anderson, Eric. A. 1989. "Economic Benefits of Habitat Restoration: Seagrass and the Virginia Hard-Shell Blue Crab Fishery." *North American Journal of Fisheries Management* 9(2):140-149.
A simple simulation model is developed to estimate economic benefits to crab fishermen and consumers. A significant relationship was found between the abundance of submerged aquatic vegetation and catch per unit of effort. Full seagrass restoration would benefit crab fishermen about $1.8 million annually and crab consumers about $2.4 million annually.

279. Anderson, Robert and Robert DeCaprio. 1992. "Banking on the Bayou." *National Wetlands Newsletter* 14(1):10.
An industry perspective on mitigation banking in Louisiana. Describes a memorandum of agreement establishing the Tenneco LaTerre wetland mitigation bank.

280. Atkinson, Robert Bolling. 1991. *An Analysis of Palustrine Forested Wetland Compensation Effectiveness in Virginia (Wetland Construction)*. Ph.D. thesis, Virginia Polytechnic Institute and State University, Blacksburg, 135 pp., (University Microfilms Inc., Order No: AAD92-08415).
Suggests a method for quantifying the effectiveness of palustrine forested wetland construction in Virginia using wetlands constructed by the Virginia Department of Transportation and the U.S. Army Corps of

Engineers as study sites. Results at four study sites suggest constructed wetland soils lack organic matter to function "properly." Elevation was also found to be an important factor in success of replacing wetland functions through construction. Does not address economic values.

* **Baker, Kimberly Anne, M. Siobhan Fennessy, and William J. Mitsch. 1991.** "Designing Wetlands for Controlling Coal Mine Drainage: An Ecologic-Economic Modelling Approach."
Cited above as entry 89.

* **Baltezore, James F., Jay A. Leitch, Sara F. Beekie, Preston F. Schutt, and Kevin. L. Grosz. 1991.** *Status of Wetlands in North Dakota in 1990.*
Cited above as entry 92.

281. **Barerndregt, A., S. M. Stam, and M. J. Wassen. 1992.** "Restoration of Fen Ecosystems in the Vecht River Plain: Cost-Benefit Analysis of Hydrological Alternatives." *Hydrobiologia* 233(1-3):247-258.
Examines 10 options for managing the Vecht River Plain (The Netherlands) where the vegetation diversity has been diminished in recent decades due to hydrological changes and resulting eutrophication. Analyzes the different options with a cost-benefit analysis. Shows how the ecological impact of various management options can be evaluated in terms of required investment. The most likely option involves recycling seepage water from the outskirts of the major polder in the plain and pumping it to the smaller outlying polders.

282. **Barnhart, E. L. 1992.** "Effluent Disposal in a Pristine Environment." *Water, Science, and Technology* 25:12,23-32.

283. **Batchelor, A., R. Bocarro, and P. J. Pybus. 1991.** "Low-Cost and Low-Energy Wastewater Treatment Systems: A South African Perspective." *Water Science and Technology* 24(5):241-246.
Presents an overview of waste treatment alternatives in South Africa. The capital construction and operating costs of constructed wetlands are similar to those of stabilization ponds, but due to lack of full scale operational information they are not yet widely used as a wastewater treatment system.

284. **Boyd, W. H. and R. L. Gray. 1992.** "Wetland Restoration, Enhancement, or Creation--A New Chapter in the USDA-SCS Engineer-

ing Field Handbook." Pp. 170-175 in *Land Reclamation: Advances in Research & Technology--Proceedings of the International Symposium*, T. Younos, P. Diplas, and S. Mostaghimi, eds., American Society of Agricultural Engineers, St. Joseph, Michigan.
A discussion of wetland restoration and creation guidelines in the USDA-SCS field handbook. Included in entry 350.

285. Breen, Bill. 1993. "To Build a Bog." *Garbage: The Practical Journal for the Environment* 5(5):32-39.
Discusses various projects in which engineers and biologists are attempting to restore or create new wetlands to replace lost ecological value of converted wetlands.

* Carey, Marc, Ralph Heimlich, and Richard Brazee. 1990. *A Permanent Wetland Reserve: Analysis of a New Approach to Wetland Protection*.
Cited above as entry 109.

286. Carlisle, Thomas, George Mulamoottil, and Bruce Mitchell. 1991. "Attitudes Towards Artificial Wetlands in Ontario for Stormwater Control and Waterfowl Habitat." *Water Resources Bulletin* 27(3):419-427.
Found that respondents' knowledge about the provision of wetlands for stormwater impoundments and waterfowl habitats was severely limited and is not considered an important management option. The overwhelming lack of this integrated approach seems to be due to a lack of understanding and its comparative newness. Recommends the design and implementation of an artificial wetland prototype as part of an education program.

287. D'Avanzo, C. 1989. "Long-term Evaluation of Wetland Creation Projects." Pp. 75-84 in *Wetland Creation and Restoration: The Status of the Science*, J. A. Kusler and M. E. Knetula, eds., U.S. Environmental Protection Agency, Corvallis, Oregon.

* Dennison, Mark S. and James F. Berry. 1993. *Wetlands: Guide to Science, Law, and Technology*.
Cited above as entry 124.

288. Doku, Isaac Adjei. 1993. *The Potential for Use of Wetlands for Wastewater Treatment in the Northwest Territories*. M.Sc. thesis,

University of Toronto, Canada, 251 pp., (University Microfilms Inc., Order No: AADMM-83489).
Reviews the current status of using wetlands for wastewater treatment. Evaluates the use of wetlands for municipal wastewater treatment in the Northwest Territories (Canada). Concludes more study is necessary to regionalize design criteria.

289. **Douglas, John H. 1992. "Constructed Wetlands Reduce Cost of Treating Acid Drainage."** *Environmental Update* **6:4-6.**

290. **Dunn, William J. 1989. "Wetland Succession--What is the Appropriate Paradigm?" Pp. 473-488 in** *Wetlands: Concerns and Successes--Proceedings of a Symposium,* **David W. Fisk, ed., American Water Resources Association, Bethesda, Maryland.**
Describes controlling factors of wetland succession, which can be typically grouped autogenic (within) or allogenic (without). Concludes, in light of new studies of created and restored wetlands, both allogenic and autogenic processes act to change wetland vegetation and single concept paradigms do not adequately explain the succession process. Included in entry 33.

291. **Ervin, David, Kenneth Algozin, Marc Carey, Otto Doering, Stephen Frerichs, Ralph Heimlich, Jim Hrubovcak, Kazim Konyar, Ian McCormick, Tim Osborn, Marc Ribaudo, and Robbin Shoemaker. 1991.** *Conservation and Environmental Issues in Agriculture: An Economic Evaluation of Policy Options.* **Staff Report AGES 9134, Resources and Technology Division, Economic Research Service, U.S. Department of Agriculture, Washington, D.C., 62 pp.**
Studies the potential economic implications of selected policy approaches to several agricultural conservation and environmental issues. Finds that new land retirement approaches targeted to wetlands restoration and to land use change for water quality and other environmental services can achieve long run environmental improvement.

292. **Erwin, Kevin L. 1992.** *Selected Bibliography: Wetland Creation and Restoration.* **Association of Wetland Managers, Inc., Berne, New York, 62 pp.**
The bibliography includes over 600 citations designed to provide researchers, practitioners, and government agencies with an index for identifying and locating publications useful in designing, evaluating, and managing wetland creation and restoration projects. Does not contain abstracts.

* **Fisk, David W., ed. 1990.** *Wetlands: Concerns and Successes--Proceedings of a Symposium.*
Cited above as entry 33.

293. **Ghosh, D. 1991. "Ecosystems Approach to Low-Cost Sanitation in India: Where the People Know Better." Pp. 63-79 in** *Ecological Engineering for Wastewater Treatment: Proceedings,* **C. Etnier, and B. Guterstam, eds., Bokskogen, Gothenburg, Sweden.**
Waterlogged areas on the edges of a number of cities in India have been identified and taken over by the government for transformation into low-cost sanitation and resource recovery ecosystems. The proposed low-cost project will transform unused or underutilized wetlands beyond the edge of a city into a cluster of ponds that will treat the sewage and use it to grow fish, using primarily solar energy. Very little institutional support has been given by the government to any of the entrepreneurs or cooperative units running this resource recovery system. Equally remarkable is the performance of a cooperative in transforming a waterlogged area into a resource-recovery ecosystem and in demonstrating a self-help sanitation model as a prototype on the southwestern fringe of Calcutta.

294. **Hammer, Donald A., ed. 1989.** *Constructed Wetlands for Wastewater Treatment.* **Lewis Publishers, Inc., Boca Raton, Florida, 800 pp.**
Contains the proceedings from the "First International Conference on Constructed Wetlands for Wastewater Treatment" held in Chattanooga, Tennessee--the first comprehensive conference on constructed wetlands for water quality improvement. This volume presents general principles of wetland ecology, hydrology, soil chemistry, vegetation, microbiology, and wildlife in chapters 1 through 7 followed by case histories of specific types of constructed wetlands and their applications in chapters 8 through 21. Chapters 22 through 36 provide construction and management guidelines beginning with policies and regulations through siting and construction and ending with operations and monitoring of constructed wetlands treatment systems. Recent theoretical and empirical results from operating systems and research facilities are included in the remaining chapters. Includes entries 328 and 335.

295. **Hammer, Donald A. 1992.** *Creating Freshwater Wetlands.* **Lewis Publishers, Inc., Boca Raton, Florida, 298 pp.**
Organizes and presents some of the information on methods to create or restore freshwater wetlands accumulated by wetland scientists and managers during the last 50 years. Introductory chapters define and classify wetlands; chapter four describes wetland functions and values, some values are quantified in dollar terms.

296. **Haynes, II, William J. and Royal C. Gardner. 1993. "The Value of Wetlands as Wetlands: The Case for Mitigation Banking."** *Environmental Law Report* **23(5):10261-10263.**
Wetlands mitigation banking offers a new approach to protecting wetlands. Article argues strongly that regulatory agencies encourage mitigation banking.

297. **Heimlich, Ralph E. 1994. "Costs of an Agricultural Wetland Reserve."** *Land Economics* **70(2):263-265.**
Eligibility and costs for wetland restoration projects were estimated using data from several large data bases. Estimated minimum costs increased from $286 million for a 1 million acre reserve to $3.8 billion for 5 million acres, drawn from 55.6 million acres of eligible cropland. The use of 8 regional bidding pools increased total costs 32 percent over a single national pool.

298. **Heimlich, Ralph E., Marc Carey, and Richard J. Brazee. 1989. "Beyond Swampbuster: A Permanent Wetland Reserve."** *Journal of Soil and Water Conservation* **44(5):445-450.**
Discusses the effectiveness of the Swampbuster Provision and analyzes the potential impact of a wetland reserve program. Found that farm program payments averaged $217 per acre idled between 1985 and 1987 and the costs of a permanent wetland reserve which would take the same land out of production would cost $1.7 billion or $337 per acre in perpetuity. Concludes that a 5 million acre wetland reserve would raise prices of major commodity crops between 3 and 7 percent by 1995. The subsequent reduction in deficiency payments would reduce government expenditures $4.3 billion over 5 years.

299. **Heimlich, Ralph. E. and D. Gadsby. 1993. "Strategies for Wetlands Protection and Restoration."** *Agricultural Outlook* **200:32-37.**
Discusses the ongoing implementation of the Wetland Reserve Program (WRP), which restores former wetlands to wetland condition. Provides tables which detail acreage accepted into the program by state. Examines the potential effects of three different wetland regulatory reform proposals: HR1330; HR350; and the Bush Administration Plan with regard to delineation, scope, permitting, mitigation banking, and coordination.

300. **Hey, D. L., M. A. Cardamone, J. H. Sather, and W. J. Mitsch. 1989. "Restoration of Riverine Wetlands: The Des Plaines River Wetlands Demonstration Project." Pp. 159-183 in** *Ecological Engineering: An Introduction to Ecotechnology,* **W. J. Mitsch and S. E. Jorgensen, eds., Wiley, New York.**

301. Howorth, Laura S. 1991. "Highway Construction and Wetland Loss: Mitigation Banking Programs in the Southeastern United States." *The Environmental Professional* 13(2):139-144.
Case studies of several southeastern states are used to illustrate potential benefits and problems associated with establishing mitigation banking programs. State programs reviewed include North Carolina, Mississippi, and Virginia. Concludes that mitigation banking has appeal to highway departments, since they have strong development interests and the task of working through the section 404 permit process.

302. Huang, Chuyu and Ziqing Ou. 1993. "Techno-Economic Analysis of Municipal Wastewater Land Treatment Systems in China." *Journal of Environmental Science-China* 5:16-22.

   * Kantrud, Harold A., Gary L. Krapu, and George A. Swanson. 1989. *Prairie Basin Wetlands of the Dakotas: A Community Profile.* Cited above as entry 169.

303. Kentula, Mary E., Robert P. Brooks, Stephanie E. Gwin, Cindy C. Holland, Arthur D. Sherman, and Jean C. Sifneos. 1993. *An Approach to Improving Decision Making in Wetland Restoration and Creation.* Ann. J. Hairston, ed., CRC Press Inc., Boca Raton, Florida, 151 pp.
Attempts to fill a gap in the information available on wetland restoration and creation by addressing how to improve future decisions by evaluating past decisions. The perspective taken was developed from the U.S. Environmental Protection Agency's Wetlands Research Program. Includes six chapters which cover the Wetlands Research Program's approach, information requirements, sampling strategies, identifying priority areas, selecting sites, defining boundaries, documentation, assessment of hydrology, morphometry, substrate, vegetation, water quality, volunteers and natural resource monitoring, representation of data, design, and other subjects.

304. Kentula, Mary E., Jean C. Sifneos, James W. Good, Michael Rylko, and Kathy Kunz. 1992. "Trends and Patterns in Section 404 Permitting Requiring Compensatory Mitigation in Oregon and Washington, USA." *Environmental Management* 16(1):109-119.
The effects of permitting decisions made under Section 404 of the Clean Water Act for which compensatory mitigation was required were examined. Information was compiled on permits issued in Oregon (January 1977-January 1987) and Washington (1980-1986). The 58 permits issued during the years of concern in Oregon document impacts to 82 wetlands

and the creation of 80. The total area of wetlands impacted was 74 ha while 42 ha were created, resulting in a net loss of 32 ha or 43 percent. The 35 permits issued in Washington document impacts to 72 wetlands and the creation of 52. The total area of wetlands impacted was 61 ha while 45 ha were created, resulting in a net loss of 16 ha or 26 percent. In both states, the number of permits requiring compensation increased with time. The area of the impacted and created wetlands tended to be ≤0.40 ha. The wetland types created most often were not always the same as those impacted; therefore, local gains and losses of certain types occurred. In both states the greatest net loss in area was in freshwater marshes.

305. **King, Dennis M. 1991. "Costing Out Restoration."** *Restoration and Management Notes* **Summer:21 (The Journal of the Society for Ecological Restoration, University of Wisconsin).**
Summarizes some problems and proposes a framework for evaluating costs and expected results of wetland restoration projects. Makes four general conclusions of the report: (1) there is currently no analytical framework for comparing cost and benefits of restoration alternatives; (2) the proposed framework incorporates most of the criteria necessary for evaluating and comparing alternatives with the exception of risk and uncertainty; (3) the framework proposed, which deals explicitly with both the cost and expected results of alternatives, is an improvement over most current methods among alternatives on the basis of subjective perfor-mance measures and imperfect cost information; and (4) since projects will be aimed at the restoration of several different ecological functions, more than one set of performance measures may be required to evaluate and compare alternatives.

306. **King, Dennis M. 1992. "Wetland Mitigation Banks--Avoiding Another Taxpayer Bailout."** *The National Wetland Newsletter* **14(1):11-12.**
Argues that until more is known about the costs of wetland creation and restoration, there is no basis for assessing when and where mitigation banks can succeed without government subsidies. Where wetland mitigation banks can work, they could help streamline the wetland permitting process and provide mitigation that is less expensive and more reliable and predictable than at present. Concludes that more attention is needed with regard to where supply and demand curves for wetland mitigation credits cross, and where they are unable to cross without a federal bailout.

307. **King, Dennis M. 1992. "Economics of Ecological Restoration."** **Pp. 493-526 in** *Natural Resource Damages: Law and Economics,*

Kevin M. Ward and John W. Duffield, eds., John Wiley and Sons, Inc., Wiley Law Publications, New York. Provides a simple analytical framework for evaluating and comparing the costs and expected performance of restoration alternatives and illustrates the process using a wetland restoration example. Also discusses wetland restoration in terms of restoration as a business, the effectiveness of restoration projects, goals, tasks, estimation of costs, and case studies. Concludes that ecological restoration is in the early stages of development, which makes it very difficult to evaluate restoration alternatives on the basis of any kind of rigorous economic analysis or "optimization" scheme. Included in entry 77.

308. **King, Dennis M., Curtis C. Bohlen, and Kenneth J. Adler. 1993.** *Watershed Management and Wetland Mitigation: A Framework for Determining Compensation Ratios.* **Office of Policy, Planning and Evaluation, U.S. Environmental Protection Agency, Washington, D.C., 16 pp.** Describes a framework for establishing wetland compensation ratios based on trading one form of environmental capital for another. Full compensation requires increases in environmental functions and values from the compensation wetland that are sufficient to make up for the decline in functions and values resulting from the loss of the existing wetland.

309. **King, Dennis M. and Curtis C. Bohlen. 1993.** *Making Sense of Wetland Restoration Costs.* **Office of Policy Analysis, U.S. Environmental Protection Agency, and the U.S. Department of Energy, Washington, D.C., 12 pp.** Explains why misperceptions about restoration costs persist, and provides baseline point and range estimates of restoration costs for various types of wetlands. These misperceptions persist because the cost of restoration projects vary widely (from $5 to $1.5 million), which does not provide very useful information. Provides average cost per acre of wetland restored for 9 different types of wetlands: aquatic bed ($19.5), complex ($56.7), freshwater mixed ($18.1), freshwater forested ($77.9), freshwater emergent ($48.7), tidal freshwater ($42.0), salt marsh ($18.1), mangroves ($18.0), and agricultural conversion ($1.0). Concludes that wetland restoration is an emerging field of applied science with very few engineering or performance standards and range of skills and experience of specialists is enormous. This is reflected in the wide range of costs and successes for most types of restoration projects.

310. **King, Dennis and Robert Costanza. 1994.** *The Cost of Wetland Creation and Restoration.* **University of Maryland Center for**

Environmental and Estuarine Studies, for U.S. Department of Energy, Pittsburgh Energy Tech. Center, Pittsburgh, Pennsylvania.

Examines the economics of wetland creation, restoration, and enhancement projects, especially as they are used within the context of mitigation. Engineering-cost-accounting profiles of over 90 wetland projects are included. Data on the costs of over 1,000 wetland projects were collected from secondary sources. Costs varied widely, ranging from $5 per acre to $1.5 million per acre. A compensation ratio concept is introduced that estimates the acres of created, restored, or enhanced wetland required to compensate for an acre of lost natural wetland.

311. Knight, Robert L. 1992. "Ancillary Benefits and Potential Problems with the Use of Wetlands for Nonpoint Source Pollution Control." *Ecological Engineering* 1(1/2):97-113.

Discusses some of the ancillary (secondary) benefits of wetlands which include (1) photosynthetic production, (2) secondary production of fauna, (3) food chain habitat and diversity, (4) export to adjacent ecosystems, and (5) aesthetic/recreational/educational human uses. Also includes some potential problems associated with wetlands utilized for NPS control: (1) conditions that are nuisance or hazardous to humans (by harboring disease, snakes, alligators, and as a toxin pathway), and (2) conditions that are hazardous to plants and wildlife (high loading of pollutants such as metals, pesticides, and other potentially toxic chemicals).

* Kraft, Steven E., Paul Dye, Andrew French, Richard Johnson, Roger Beck, and Dennis Robinson. 1991. "Preservation and Restoration of Wetland: The Challenge of Economic-Ecological Input/Output Modeling."
Cited above as entry 46.

* Kusler, Jon A., Sally Daly, and Gail Brooks, eds. 1988. *Proceedings of the National Wetland Symposium: Urban Wetlands.*
Cited above as entry 48.

* Kusler, Jon A. and Sally Daly, eds. 1989. *Wetlands and River Corridor Management: Proceedings of an International Symposium.*
Cited above as entry 177.

312. Kusler, Jon A. and Mary E. Kentula, eds. 1989. *Wetland Creation and Restoration: The Status of the Science.* Volumes I and II, U.S. Environmental Protection Agency, Corvallis, Oregon, 473 pp.

Volume I contains regional reviews of attempts to compensate for wetland losses by creating new wetlands or restoring degraded ones. Synthesizes the knowledge accumulated to date into a statement on the status of the science of wetland creation and restoration. Identifies limits of knowledge and attempts to set priorities for future research. Volume II contains a series of theme papers covering a wide range of topics of general application to wetland creation and restoration (hydrology, management, planning).

* Kusler, Jon A. and Richard Smardon, eds. 1990. *Wetlands of the Great Lakes: Protection and Restoration Policies--Status of the Science.*
Cited above as entry 178.

313. Lan, Chongyu, Guizhu Chen, Liuchun Li, and M. H. Wong. 1992. "Use of Cattails in Treating Wastewater From a Pb/Zn Mine." *Environmental Management* 16(1):75-80.
Describes the use of a combined treatment system, which includes an aquatic treatment pond with *Typha latifolia* and a stabilization pond to treat wastewater from a lead/zinc mine in China. *T. latifolia* assimilated significant amounts of lead and zinc, especially in the root portion.

* Landin, Mary C., ed. 1993. *Wetlands: Proceedings of the 13th Annual Conference, Society of Wetland Scientists, New Orleans, Louisiana.*
Cited above as entry 49.

* Lant, Christopher and Steven E. Kraft. 1993. *An Evaluation of Policy Tools to Establish Forests and Protect Water Quality in Cornbelt Watersheds.*
Cited above as entry 182.

314. Lee, B. and L. Stuber. 1991. "Wetland Treatment System Feasibility Study." Pp. 255-258 in *Proceedings of the 1991 Georgia Water Resources Conference, Athens, Georgia, March 19-20, 1991,* K. J. Hatcher, ed., University of Georgia, Athens.

315. Lewis, Roy R. 1992. "Why Florida Needs Mitigation Banking." *National Wetlands Newsletter* 14(1):7.
Claims that the recent "failure" of Florida wetlands mitigation lies not within the concept of the bank itself, but rather the lack of a "wetland policy" to ensure compliance. Recommends advancement of the science of wetlands restoration and creation.

316. **Marble, Anne D. 1992.** *A Guide to Wetland Functional Design.* **Lewis Publishing, Inc., Boca Raton, Florida, 222 pp.**
Presents a conceptual approach to wetland design from a functional standpoint, based on the Wetland Evaluation Technique (WET). Site selection and site design features for wetland replacement are described for nutrient removal/transformation, sediment/toxicant retention, shoreline stabilization, floodflow alteration, groundwater recharge, production export, aquatic diversity and abundance, and wetland dependent bird habitat diversity. The design of multiple functions is also discussed.

317. **Marsh, Lindell L. and Dennis R. Acker. 1992. "Mitigation Banking on a Wider Plane."** *National Wetlands Newsletter* **14(1):8-9.**
Discusses mitigation banking and highlights two issues which have significantly affected their use. The first regards the extent to which mitigation banks should provide credits for conserving wetlands that are different from the kind of wetland to be impacted. The second issue is whether mitigation should appear in the same watershed or within a fixed distance of the impacted watersheds.

318. **McComas, Steve. 1994.** *Lake Smarts: The First Lake Maintenance Handbook.* **Terrene Institute, Washington, D.C., 228 pp.**
Describes over 100 techniques to improve the water quality and wildlife values of water bodies. A layperson's how-to manual addressing a range of ecological situations, including wetlands.

319. **McCorvie, Mary R. and Christopher L. Lant. 1993. "Drainage District Formation and the Loss of Midwestern Wetlands, 1850-1930."** *Agricultural History* **67(4):13-49.**
Outlines the history of wetland conversion with regard to policy initiatives. Discusses various reasons for converting wetlands, including provision of arable land, land speculation, and fear of malaria. Shows how the subsequent establishment of drainage districts and canals block more recent efforts to restore wetlands.

320. **McCrain, Gerald Ray. 1990.** *Habitat Evaluation Procedures (HEP) Applied to Mitigation Banking in North Carolina (Wetlands).* **Ph.D. thesis, North Carolina State University, Raleigh, 97 pp., (University Microfilms Inc., Order No: AAD91-12179).**
Evaluates functional value replacement using Habitat Evaluation Procedure (HEP) at 15 highway sites in North Carolina. Concludes that acre-for-acre mitigation is insufficient for functional value replacement. Recommends a three-to-one replacement ratio for bottomland hardwood wetland losses.

321. Mitsch, William J., Jingsong Yau, and Julie K. Cronk. 1993. "Ecological Engineering: Contrasting Experiences in China and the West." *Ecological Engineering* (2):177-191.
Discusses some of the differences between western and Chinese systems which relate to design principles, objectives, human manipulation of ecosystem structure, and recognized values and economics.

322. Mitsch, William. J. and Julie. K. Cronk. 1992. "Creation and Restoration of Wetlands: Some Design Consideration for Ecological Engineering." *Advances in Soil Science* 17:217-259.
Discusses a wide range of topics regarding wetland creation and restoration with an emphasis on wetland design. Provides costs of constructed wetlands for various uses in the U.S. Construction costs reported vary from $2.53/m^2$ for a dredged material disposal site in Virginia to $208.00/m^2$ for an artifical wetland for wastewater treatment in Pennsylvania, with an average of $37.48/m^2$ for 14 sites. Concludes that costs of constructed wetlands are available and tend to be quite site specific; maintenance costs and economic benefits are even more difficult to estimate.

323. Owen, Catherine Rutherford. 1993. *Policy-Relevant Science: Hydrologic Functions of an Urban Wetland (Groundwater, Land Use, Wetland)*. Ph.D. thesis, University of Wisconsin, Madison, 228 pp., (University Microfilms Inc., Order No: AAD93-09526).
Assesses groundwater recharge and storm runoff retention functions of a palustrine peatland wetland in Wisconsin. Very little hydrologic exchange between the wetland and the groundwater or an adjacent watercourse was found. Presents some wetland restoration management options for replacing functions.

324. Parks, P. J. and R. A. Kramer. 1991. "Costs of Wetlands Protection and Restoration Policies: Positive and Normative Approaches." Pp. 12-17 in *A National Policy of "No Net Loss" of Wetlands: What do Agricultural Economists Have to Contribute?* Ralph E. Heimlich, ed., Staff Report No. AGES 9149, Resources and Technology Division, Economic Research Service, U.S. Department of Agriculture, Washington, D.C.
Examines the potential effectiveness of a policy similar to the Conservation Reserve Program in the context of wetland protection. Concludes (1) positive studies of wetland policy costs are scarce, and (2) heterogeneity of land and of owners must be considered in analyzing wetland policies. Included in entry 153.

325. **Redmond, Ann. 1992. "How Successful is Mitigation?"** *National Wetlands Newsletter* **14(1):5-6.**
Reports on a recent study of 119 wetland creation projects in Florida that shows that many required projects have not been conducted, and less than half of the completed mitigation projects are ecologically successful. Concludes that there is a need for stronger emphasis on permit compliance and enforcement in order to improve the success rate of wetland mitigation projects.

326. **Reppert, R. 1992.** *Wetlands Mitigation Banking Concepts.* **Report 92-WMB-1, Institute for Water Resources, U.S. Army Corps of Engineers, Ft. Belvoir, Virginia, 25 pp.**
Provides general background information on wetlands mitigation banking. Part of a two-phase effort which began in 1991 to review and evaluate banks, analyze technical and policy issues, assess credit and debit methods, and determine feasibility of a wetland mitigation banking demonstration program.

327. **Roberts, Leslie. 1993. "Wetlands Trading is a Loser's Game, Say Ecologists."** *Science* **260(5116):1890-1892.**
Claim that wetland mitigation products that began in the 1980s have not been successful because of the many gaps in wetland ecology which have not permitted the construction of a functioning ecosystem.

328. **Sather, J. H. 1989. "Ancillary Benefits of Wetlands Constructed Primarily for Wastewater Treatment."** **Pp. 353-358 in** *Constructed Wetlands for Wastewater Treatment,* **Donald A. Hammer, ed., Lewis Publishers, Inc., Boca Raton, Florida.**
Included in entry 294.

329. **Shabman, Leonard. 1991.** *A Policy Strategy for Maintaining and Rehabilitating Chesapeake Bay's Nontidal Wetlands.* **Paper prepared for AAAS Annual Meeting, Washington, D.C., Virginia Polytechnic Institute, Blacksburg, 6 pp.**
Recommends a centralized alternative system for management of wetlands, one which moves in the direction of "share the gain" decision rule.

330. **Shabman, Leonard. 1991. "Integrating Reconversion of Wetlands into Achieving Environmental Goals in Urbanizing Regions."** **Pp. 23-28 in** *A National Policy of "No Net Loss" of Wetlands: What do Agricultural Economists Have to Contribute?* **Ralph E. Heimlich, ed., Staff Report No. AGES 9149, Resources and**

Technology Division, Economic Research Service, U.S. Department of Agriculture, Washington, D.C.
Included in entry 153.

331. Shabman, Leonard, Dennis King, and Paul Scodari. 1993. "Wetland Mitigation Success Through Credit Market Systems." *Wetland Journal* 5(2):9-12.
Points out the benefits of a mitigation credit market alternative to enhance the ability of compensatory mitigation to serve the no-net-loss and net gain goals.

332. Shabman, Leonard, Dennis King, and Paul Scodari. 1993. *Making Wetlands Mitigation Work: The Credit Market Alternative.* Staff Paper SP-93-5, Department of Agricultural and Applied Economics, Virginia Tech, Blacksburg, 62 pp.
A more extensive version of entries 331 and 333.

333. Shabman, Leonard, Paul Scodari, and Dennis King. 1994. *Expanding Opportunities for Successful Wetland Mitigation: The Private Credit Market Alternative.* Institute for Water Resources, U.S. Army Corps of Engineers, Ft. Belvoir, Virginia, 9 pp.
Describes the potential for private markets in mitigation credits to help the federal wetland regulatory program achieve the national goal of no-net-loss in wetland function and acreage, and explains the regulatory conditions necessary for their widespread emergence and ecological success.

334. Shelton, Paul Alan. 1992. *Productivity and Waterfowl Utilization of Surface Mine Wetlands and Impoundments.* Ph.D. thesis, Southern Illinois University, Carbondale, (University Microfilms Inc., Order No: AAD94-03415).
Relationships between environmental factors, primary and secondary productivity, and waterfowl use were assessed at the Peabody Coal Company Will Scarlet Mine in southern Illinois. Additions of sewage sludge to wetlands had variable effects depending on season.

335. Smardon, R. C. 1989. "Human Perception of Utilization of Wetlands for Waste Assimilation, or How Do You Make a Silk Purse Out of a Sow's Ear." Pp. 287-295 in *Constructed Wetlands for Wastewater Treatment,* Donald A. Hammer, ed., Lewis Publishers, Inc., Boca Raton, Florida.
Included in entry 294.

* Smit, H. and H. Coops. 1991. "Ecological, Economic and Social Aspects of Natural and Man-made Bulrush *Scirpus lacustris L.* Wetlands in The Netherlands."
Cited above as entry 225.

336. Smith, L. Graham, Thomas J. Carlisle, and Sonya N. Meek. 1993. "Implementing Sustainability: The Use of Natural Channel Design and Artificial Wetlands for Stormwater Management." *Journal of Environmental Management* 37(4):241-257.
Provides a discussion of sustainability and the application of the concept to the management of water resources. Illustrates how the concept can be used for urban stormwater management and planning. Concludes by offering research opportunities to investigate the feasibility of adopting natural channel design and artificial wetlands for sustainable stormwater management.

337. U.S. Department of Agriculture. 1993. *1992 Wetlands Reserve Program: Report to Congress.* Washington, D.C., 22 pp.
Summarizes current operations and progress of the 1992 pilot Wetlands Reserve Program (WRP). The fiscal year 1992 appropriations bill for the Department of Agriculture (P.L. 102-142) provided $46.357 million for WRP. On January 14, 1993, 239 bids for 49,888 acres from 265 farms were tentatively accepted into the program; study includes breakdown of costs.

338. U.S. Environmental Protection Agency. 1990. *The Economics of Improved Estuarine Water Quality: An NEP Manual for Measuring Benefits.* Office of Marine and Estuarine Protection, Office of Policy, Planning, and Evaluation, U.S. Environmental Protection Agency, Washington, D.C., 62 pp.
Designed to assist estuary program managers and staff in determining the cost effectiveness of various pollution abatement options. Explains the concept of economic benefits, then describes how abatement projects can generate benefits. Gives detailed procedures for defining and estimating recreational, as well as commercial fishing benefits.

339. U.S. General Accounting Office. 1991. *Wetlands Preservation: Easements are Protecting Prairie Potholes but Some Improvements are Possible.* GAO/RCED-92-27, Gaithersburg, Maryland, 18 pp.
Reports on an assessment of the Fish and Wildlife Service's wetland easement program in four FWS wetland management districts. Concludes

that easements are protecting prairie potholes and that almost all damaged wetlands under easement are restored to productive habitat.

340. **U.S. Prairie Pothole Joint Venture Implementation Plan. 1989.** *U.S. Prairie Pothole Joint Venture for Wildlife and People.* **U.S. Fish and Wildlife Service, Denver and Minneapolis, 59 pp.**
A component of the North American Waterfowl Management Plan. Identifies management strategies of the Prairie Pothole region with the goal of involving the public in a broad-scale united effort to increase waterfowl by preserving, restoring, creating, and enhancing wildlife habitat. Mentions establishing wetland values in order to develop and sustain wetland habitat on private land.

341. **van der Valk, Arnold G. and Robert W. Jolly. 1992. "Recommendations for Research to Develop Guidelines for the Use of Wetlands to Control Rural Nonpoint Source Pollution."** *Ecological Engineering* **1(1/2):115-134.**
States that some major technical issues need to be resolved before effective and realistic guidelines can be developed for using restored wetlands to reduce NPS pollution: (1) effects of contaminants on restored wetlands, (2) fate of organic compounds, (3) site selection, (4) landowner cooperation, (5) who pays for restorations, and (6) how cost effective is this approach. Recommends implementing studies to determine the economic costs and benefits to rural NPS pollution reduction and how costs associated with its reduction can be internalized.

342. **Vietinghoff, U., H. Puta, H. Klapper, M. Stender, and M. L. Hubert. 1990. "Ecosystem Management in Estuaries: Costs and Benefits."** *Limnologica* **20:157-163.**
Describes two computer-based methods designed to assist decision making regarding estuary restoration. Presents a short list of restoration methods for eutrophied estuaries. Differentiates between processes that cause costs, and processes that lead to benefits; all elementary processes of restoration are expressed in monetary terms. The ecological processes are qualitatively described by mathematical models. In order to find the restoration that shows the best ecological results connected with a minimum of costs, a scenario analyses and optimization techniques (variable metric method) are applied.

343. **Walter, John. 1991. "Corn Coexists with Wetlands."** *Successful Farming* **89(11):36.**
Roger and Tim Tarr, father and son, deepened an abandoned stream bed on their farm to create twelve wetland acres. The wetlands attract migrat-

ing waterfowl and other wildlife. The Tarrs report little bird-related crop damage.

344. **Walter, John. 1992. "What Value Wetlands?"** *Successful Farming* **90(9):25.**
According to research, recent restoration of wetlands has not made the best use of water quality benefits.

345. **Wenzel, Thomas A. 1992.** *Minnesota Wetland Restoration Guide.* **Minnesota Board of Water and Soil Resources, St. Paul.**
A reference guidebook for planning, surveying, design, construction, and maintenance of wetland restoration projects. Intended primarily for use in Minnesota. Typical of wetland restoration/creation literature--extols wetlands' many values without quantifying them. In the seven-page section on planning, the author notes, "The cost-benefit aspect of restoring a wetland is very difficult to determine. These and other questions need to be answered by local professionals who are familiar with the projects and the areas in which they are located."

346. **Whitaker, G. and C. R. Terrell. 1992. "Federal Programs for Wetland Restoration and Use of Wetlands for Non-point Source Pollution Control."** *Ecological Engineering* **1(1-2):157-170.**
A review of federal wetlands programs in the U.S. shows that a number of agencies have made significant wetland restoration and creation efforts. Water quality improvement is not the main objective of most of these programs, and areas with high nonpoint source (NPS) pollution may actually be avoided in order to protect wetland values such as habitat. However, ancillary water quality benefits are provided by many created and restored wetlands, and agencies such as the U.S. Department of Agriculture are actively evaluating the use of created and restored wetlands as components of NPS control strategies.

347. **White, Timothy A., Charles L. Blair, and Keith B. MacDonald. 1992. "Wetland Replacement: The Art and Science of Renewing Damaged Ecosystems."** *Renewable Resources Journal* **10(4):18-24.**
Puts the wetland replacement issue in perspective by discussing types and functions, the mitigation controversy, forms of mitigation, project planning, limitations to wetland replacement, banking, and the role of agricultural policy.

348. **Wilder, L. 1987. "Mississippi Farmers Value Wetlands."** *The Service* **8(8):6-8.**

Interviews three Mississippi farmers who put some of their farmed wetlands back to wetlands. They describe the positive functions of wetlands, economic values and advocate a stricter wetlands provision act.

349. **Wong, Mei Yee. 1993.** *A Profile of Nonpoint Source Pollutants in the Palo Alto Area and the Feasibility of Constructing Wetlands as a Treatment Option.* **M.S. thesis, San Jose State University, California, 76 pp., (University Microfilms Inc., Order No: AAD13-54174).**

Concludes it is feasible to construct wetlands to treat runoff to reduce loads reaching San Francisco Bay.

350. **Younos, T. M., P. Diplas, and S. Mostaghimi, eds. 1992.** *Land Reclamation: Advances in Research & Technology.* **Proceedings of the International Symposium, American Society of Agricultural Engineers, St. Joseph, Michigan, 381 pp.**

Contains 44 papers presented at a land reclamation conference. Topics covered include development and applications of computer models, geographical information systems, remote sensing technology, salinity problems, surface and groundwater monitoring, wetland restoration techniques, and land use planning for resource protection. Includes entry 284.

WETLAND DELINEATION/ DEFINITION ISSUES

OVERVIEW

Wetland definition and delineation remains the single most problematic social and technical aspect of developing effective and efficient wetland management policies. Scarce literature exists on the direct economic consequences of alternative wetland delineation policies, yet there is an abundance of press in the popular media about delineation and definition and the problems they cause. The *National Wetlands Newsletter* is a good periodic source for keeping up with the latest definition and delineation issues from a legislative perspective.

This section includes enough of the delineation literature to gain an appreciation for the issues. It does not include reference to many of the scores of Congressional hearings, reports, and documents; the unpublished reports of the federal agencies; nor the grey literature of state agencies. Several inventory and status of wetlands reports are included, since the results of inventories are directly related to the definition of what is being inventoried.

Two references that provide a comprehensive overview of definition and delineation issues are CAST's (1994) *Wetland Policy Issues* and Environmental Defense Fund's (1992) *How Wet is a Wetland?*

REFERENCES

CAST. 1994. *Wetland Policy Issues.* Council for Agricultural Science and Technology, Ames Iowa.

Environmental Defense Fund and World Wildlife Fund. 1992. *How Wet is a Wetland? The Impacts of the Proposed Revisions to the Federal Wetlands Delineation Manual.* Environmental Defense Fund and World Wildlife Fund, Washington, D.C.

SELECTED BIBLIOGRAPHY

351. Agovino, A. Vincent. 1990. "Wetland Identification: A Means to Prevent Potential Public Health Problems." *Journal of Environmental Health* 52(5):280-281.
Development pressures across the U.S., especially in the Northeast, have focused public attention on the protection and preservation of wetlands. Installation of on-site sewage disposal systems in hydric soils may adversely affect public health. Although most health departments are not responsible for enforcing regulations related to wetlands, an understanding of wetlands and their characteristics will help the sanitarian or environmental health specialist who is reviewing site development applications to anticipate and eliminate potential problems before they occur.

352. Alper, J. 1990. "War Over the Wetland-Ecologist vs. the White House." *Science* 257(5073):1043-1044.
Discusses Vice President Dan Quayle's Council on Competitiveness modifying regulations for wetlands that would protect only areas that are wet continuously. Expands on different strategies of categorizing wetlands, such as the "patch dynamics" paradigm.

353. Anderson, John and Maurits Roos. 1991. *Using Digital Scanned Aerial Photography for Wetlands Delineation.* Earth and Atmospheric Remote Sensing Conference, SPIE Symposium on Optical Engineering and Photonics in Aerospace Engineering, Orlando, Florida.
Presents techniques used to scan (digitize), archive, and utilize digital aerial photography for environmental resource management using a photogrammetrically accurate, CCD-based scanner. Spectral characteristics of the imagery and useful image processing routines to enhance the resulting raster file(s) for interpretation are discussed.

354. Association of Bay Area Governments. 1991. *Status and Trends Report on Wetlands and Related Habitats in the San Francisco Estuary.* U.S. Fish and Wildlife Service and Romberg Tiburon Centers, San Francisco State University, San Francisco.

355. Atkinson, R. B., J. E. Perry, E. Smith, and J. Carns, Jr. 1993. "Use of Created Wetland Delineation and Weighted Averages as a Component of Assessment." *Wetlands* 13(3):185-193.
Tests hypotheses that one parameter (vegetation) could be used to evaluate early site conditions following wetland creation. Attempts to

show the advantages and disadvantages of using vegetation to calculate percentage "wetland" and "upland" as an early monitoring tool. Found vegetation colonizing the site may respond to soil and hydrology and may provide an early indication of conditions within created wetlands. Findings suggest that calculating plot-weighted averages and comparisons with pre-impact wetland vegetation (or an adjacent reference wetland) may be useful components of a monitoring scheme for certain created wetlands.

356. **Auble, Gregor T. and Elizabeth W. Bookman. 1993. "Normal Years in Wetland Delineation." Pp. 730-734 in** *Wetlands: Proceedings of the 13th Annual Conference, Society of Wetland Scientists, New Orleans, Louisiana,* **Mary C. Landin, ed., Society of Wetland Scientists, South Central Chapter, Utica, Mississippi.**
Applies the proposed requirements for years of normal rainfall to some long-term precipitation records to determine what fraction of years would allow use of on-site hydrologic observations as described in The Federal Manual for Identifying and Delineating Jurisdictional Wetlands. The results of this analysis emphasize a need to consider variability when relating hydrologic conditions to wetland structure and functions. Included in entry 49.

* **Aust, W. M., S. F. Mader, L. J. Mitchell, and R. Lea. 1990. "An Approach to the Inventory of Forested Wetlands for Timber-Harvesting Impact Assessment."**
Cited above as entry 88.

357. **Berger, Warren. 1992. "Drowning in Wetlands Rules."** *Real Estate Today* **25:6,18-22.**
Wetlands regulations and legislation are in a state of change, causing a great deal of confusion in the real estate industry. Agents and developers are losing time, effort, and land value because the rules are constantly reinterpreted.

358. **Bohlen, Curtis C. 1991. "Controversy Over Federal Definition of Wetlands."** *BioScience* **41(3):139.**
Outlines wetland controversy nationally and within Dorchester County, Maryland.

359. **Bradford, Hazel and Debra K. Rubin. 1991. "New Definitions Prompt Whole New Controversy."** *Environment and Natural Resources* **226(21):12.**

360. Bradley, J. B. and D. B. Simons. 1990. "Delineation of Ordinary High Water." Pp. 1164-1167 in *Hydraulic Engineering: Proceedings of the 1990 National Conference*, American Society of Civil Engineers, New York.

361. Bridgham, S. D., S. P. Faulkner, and C. J. Richardson. 1991. "Steel Rod Oxidation as a Hydrologic Indicator in Wetland Soils." *Soil Science Society of America Journal* 55(3):856-862.
Proposes the use of rusting steel rods as an inexpensive means of determining the depth of the water table and the reducing zone in wetland soils. Although the method was successful for relatively constant hydrologic conditions, it is unsuitable for jurisdictional purposes in fluctuating hydrologic conditions due to prolonged lag periods in rod oxidation under some conditions and the inability of previously formed rust to dissolve upon reflooding.

362. Broomhall, D. E. and W. R. Kearns. 1992. *The Status of Wetlands Management in Virginia*. Land: Issues and Problems, No. 78, Cooperative Extension Service, Virginia Tech., Blacksburg, 4 pp.

363. Bunkley, William and Charles P. Edmonds III. 1992. "Appraising Wetlands." *The Appraisal Journal* 60:107-112.
Presents a real estate appraisal perspective of the wetland delineation issue. Confusion about wetlands is making the determination of property value difficult because a great deal of uncertainty exists about how wetlands are defined. Uncertainty about wetland definitions may also cause substantial reductions in property values.

364. Burd, F. 1989. *Saltmarsh Survey of Great Britain: An Inventory of British Saltmarshes*. Research and Survey in Nature Conservation No. 17, Nature Conservancy Council, Peterborough, United Kingdom, 180 pp.
Presents several workers' research, who have, over seven years, located and mapped all the saltmarsh sites in the United Kingdom using a vegetation classification system specifically designed for this project. Results are presented as a main report, regional supplements, and county reports. The survey does not attempt to make value judgements on individual sites, but does allow an informed assessment of the site to be made in relation to the rest of the British resource.

* Burling, James S. 1992. "Property Rights, Endangered Species, Wetlands, and Other Critters: Is it Against Nature to Pay for a Taking?"
Cited above as entry 107.

365. **Busch, W. Dieter N. and Peter G. Sly. 1992.** *The Development of an Aquatic Habitat Classification System for Lakes.* **CRC Press, Boca Raton, Florida, 240 pp.**
Includes review and presentation of published habitat criteria reports by six teams, presentation of applied case studies by four teams, and a workshop combined to develop an aquatic habitat classification system. Includes entry 408.

366. **Canalos, Chris, Rob Robinson, and Jim Durana. 1992. "Classifying Land Cover for Wetlands: A First Step in Statewide Wetlands Monitoring."** **Vol. 1:1-260(3) in** *Australian Remote Sensing 6th Conference Proceedings,* **Wellington, New Zealand.**

367. **Carter, Virginia. 1994. "Ecotone Dynamics and Boundary Determination in the Great Dismal Swamp."** *Ecological Applications* **4:189-203.**
Selects tentative wetland boundary through ordination analysis of four transects across the 48-km wetland to upland transition zone of the Great Dismal Swamp of Virginia/North Carolina using data on hydrogeology, soils, and vegetation.

368. **Carter, Virginia, Mary Keith Garrett, and Patricia T. Gammon. 1988. "Wetland Boundary Determination in the Great Dismal Swamp Using Weighted Averages."** *Water Resources Bulletin* **24(2):297-306.**
Uses weighted averages to determine if a more uniform determination of wetland boundaries can be made nationwide. Found that the method used did not provide for objective placement of an absolute wetland boundary, but did serve to focus attention on the transitional boundary zone where supplementary information is necessary to select a wetland-upland breakpoint.

369. **Cashin, G. E., J. R. Dorney, and C. J. Richardson. 1992. "Wetland Alteration Trends on the North Carolina Coastal Plain."** *Wetlands* **12(2):63-71.**
Assesses wetland alterations defined by their functions and values between pre-settlement, the early 1950s, and the early 1980s on 27 randomly selected sample sites.

370. **Coats, Robert and Lee MacDonald. 1988. "Use of Hydrologic Criteria in Wetland Delineation."** **Pp. 164-172 in** *Proceedings of the National Wetland Symposium: Urban Wetlands,* **Jon A.**

Kusler, Sally Daly, and Gail Brooks, eds., Association of Wetland Managers, Inc., Berne, New York.
Discusses a number of quantitative hydrologic methods to delineate and characterize wetlands. Included in entry 48.

371. **Cox, Chris. 1992. "Satellite Imagery, Aerial Photography and Wetland Archaeology."** *World Archaeology* **24(2):249-267.**
The Northwest Wetlands Survey is undertaking extensive field survey over seven counties of northwest England. Satellite imagery and aerial photographic evidence has been analytically compared and combined to define and classify peat deposits and associated wetlands in Cumbria, England. This pilot study has devised new ways of enhancing satellite imagery which are suitable for the classification of lowland wetlands.

372. **Dahl, Thomas E. 1990.** *Wetlands Losses in the United States 1780s to 1980s.* **Fish and Wildlife Service, U.S. Department of the Interior, Washington, D.C., 21 pp.**
Presents statistics on estimated wetland loss for a 200-year timespan. Estimates 103.3 million acres remain in the U.S. as of the mid 1980s. This represents a 53 percent decrease since the birth of the U.S.

373. **Dahl, Thomas E., Craig E. Johnson, and W. E. Frayer. 1991.** *Wetlands Status and Trends in the Conterminous United States, Mid-1970's to Mid-1980's.* **Fish and Wildlife Service, U.S. Department of the Interior, Washington, D.C., 22 pp.**
This report is the first update of an earlier report titled *Status and Trends of Wetlands and Deepwater Habitats in the Conterminous United States, 1950's to 1970's*, which was completed in 1982. It constitutes a statistically rigorous effort to estimate the nation's wetland resources and provide indications of gains or losses for 14 categories of wetland and deepwater habitats.

* **Douglas, Aaron J. and Richard L. Johnson. 1994. "Drainage Investment and Wetlands Loss: An Analysis of the Resources Inventory Data."**
Cited above as entry 128.

374. **Dubensky, Mitch. 1990. "Wetlands Regulations--Beware the Net."** *Tree Farmer* **p. 12.**
Recommends that tree farmers properly comply with government guidelines on wetland activities or "Best Management Practices." Criticizes the U.S. government's policy on wetland delineation and laments the regulations of Section 404.

375. **Environmental Defense Fund and World Wildlife Fund. 1992.** *How Wet is a Wetland? The Impacts of the Proposed Revisions to the Federal Wetlands Delineation Manual.* **Environmental Defense Fund and World Wildlife Fund, Washington, D.C., 175 pp.**
Criticizes the proposed 1991 revisions to federal wetland delineation. Provides a brief background to the delineation issue. Identifies wetlands excluded by the 1991 proposed revisions. Describes impacts of revisions on regulation of selected wetlands including prairie potholes, Everglades, Chesapeake Bay, San Francisco estuary, Louisiana hardwood forests, Verde River wetlands, and willow wetlands of the Rocky Mountains. Concludes that the 1989 manual could benefit from technical refinement and clarification, but the 1991 revisions would create more problems than they would eliminate.

376. **Environmental Laboratory. 1987.** *Corps of Engineers Wetland Delineation Manual.* **Technical Report Y-87-1, Waterways Experiment Station, U.S. Army Corps of Engineers, Vicksburg, Mississippi, 100 pp.**
The "1987 Federal Manual" for wetland delineation.

377. **Federal Interagency Committee for Wetland Delineation. 1989.** *Federal Manual for Identifying and Delineating Jurisdictional Wetlands.* **Cooperative Technical Publication, U.S. Army Corps of Engineers, U.S. Environmental Protection Agency, U.S. Fish and Wildlife Service, and U.S. Soil Conservation Service, Washington, D.C., 76 pp.**
The "1989 Federal Manual" for wetland delineation.

378. **Ferguson, Nancy M. and Karen Clement-Smith. 1988.** "A Computerized Database for the Marin County, California Bay Shoreline." **Pp. 145-152 in** *Proceedings of the National Wetland Symposium: Urban Wetlands,* **Jon A. Kusler, Sally Daly, and Gail Brooks, eds., Association of Wetland Managers, Inc., Berne, New York.**
Discusses the development of a computerized database as a tool for making decisions about wetlands, related uplands, and diked baylands in Marin County, California. Included in entry 48.

379. **Finlayson, Max and Michael Moser. 1991.** *Wetlands.* **International Waterfowl and Wetlands Research Bureau, Slimbridge, Gloucester, United Kingdom, 224 pp.**
Represents the culmination of more than 20 years of work to document the status of the world's major wetlands. The first chapter defines

wetlands and their values; the remaining chapters consist of a region-by-region look at the world's wetlands.

380. **Fornshell, Donna Jean. 1992.** *Identification of Wetlands in Noxubee County, Mississippi: A Hydroclimatologic, Thematic Mapper, and GIS Analysis.* **M.S. thesis, Mississippi State University, Mississippi State, 101 pp., (University Microfilms Inc., Order No: AAD13-53350).**
Develops a method for wetland identification using satellite imagery. Coincidence of wetland identification with the National Wetlands Inventory maps on three approaches was 77 percent, 72 percent, and 63 percent.

381. **Foy, G. 1990. "Oil and Gas Activity and Louisiana Wetland Loss."** *Journal of Environmental Management* **31(3):289-297.**
Uses two methods to estimate the contribution of oil and gas activity in the Louisiana coastal zone and federal outer continental shelf region to Louisiana wetland loss in the period 1955-1980: (1) wetland scientists' consensus estimates, and (2) a time series model to determine the marginal oil and gas related wetland loss per thousand barrels of oil-gas equivalent and per well. A comparison of the results of the two methods provides a check on their reliability in an area of scientific uncertainty.

382. **Frayer, W. E. and J. M. Hefner. 1991.** *Florida Wetlands--Status and Trends, 1970's to 1980's.* **Southeast Region, U.S. Fish and Wildlife Service, Atlanta, Georgia, 31 pp.**
Examines wetland changes that occurred from the mid-1970's to the mid-1980's. Also provides estimates of losses, gains, and current status of Florida's wetlands and deep water habitats.

383. **Gebhard, Robin L. 1988. "The National Wetlands Inventory." Pp. 142-144 in** *Proceedings of the National Wetland Symposium: Urban Wetlands,* **Jon A. Kusler, Sally Daly, and Gail Brooks. eds., Association of Wetland Managers, Inc., Berne, New York.**
Presents an overview of the National Wetlands Inventory mapping procedures and digital database development. Included in entry 48.

384. **Gi-Chul, Yi, David Risley, Mark Koneff, and Craig Davis. 1994. "Development of Ohio's GIS-based Wetlands Inventory."** *Journal of Soil and Water Conservation* **49:23-28.**
Discusses the advantages of Geographic Information System (GIS) natural resource management over the previous national wetlands inventory maps. Concluded that, if properly used, the GIS will give the state of Ohio the capability to periodically monitor its wetland resources.

* Gray, Jerry. 1992. "Tax Judge Lowers Assessment of Undeveloped Wetlands Tract."
Cited above as entry 143.

385. **Gren, Ing-Marie. 1993. "Alternative Nitrogen Reduction Policies in the Mälar Region, Sweden."** *Ecological Economics* **7:159-172.**
The load of nitrogen to the Stockholm archipelago from the Mälar region, a drainage basin located on the east coast of Sweden, must be reduced in order to decrease eutrophication. Costs for two alternative nitrogen policies are estimated: (1) current policy defined as total costs for reducing the nitrogen emission at each source by 50 percent, and (2) an alternative policy defined as the minimum cost for reducing the load of nitrogen to the Stockholm archipelago by 50 percent. Results demonstrate that the cost of the first alternative greatly exceeds the cost for the second alternative. One important reason is that in the second alternative the functioning of the Mälar lake ecosystem as a nitrogen sink is accounted for, which implies cost savings since less man-made reduction is required at the emission sources. Another factor is the identification of a new ecological technology--restoration of wetlands--a low cost measure for reducing the load of nitrogen.

386. **Grumbles, Benjamin H. 1994. "Wetlands Debate Still Far From Over."** *Environmental Protection* **5:33-38.**
Discusses some of the wetland proposals facing the 103rd Congress in 1994, primarily the delineation aspects. Characterizes the situation as "gridlock." Common themes are improved wetland science, regionalization, and watershed-based approaches.

387. **Hanley, Thomas. 1992. "A Developer's Dream: The United States Claims Court's New Analysis of Section 404 Takings Challenges."** *Boston College Environmental Affairs Law Review* **19(2):317-353.**
Criticizes the U.S. Claims Court consideration of section 404 cases. By refusing to consider environmental interests, by unduly restricting its economic impact analysis, and by disregarding even unreasonable investment-backed expectations the Claims Court skewed its analysis unduly in favor of the private developer.

388. **Hefner, J. M. and C. G. Storrs. 1991. "Delineation and Classification of Wetlands in the Southeast."** *The Station* **68:69-72.**
Paper presented at the symposium "Ecological Land Classification: Applications to Identify the Productive Potential of Southern Forest" (Southeast Forest Experiment Station, Forest Service, U.S. Department of Agriculture, Asheville, North Carolina).

389. Heimlich, Ralph. E. 1991. "New Wetland Definition Debated."
     Agricultural Outlook AO-180:22-25.
     A chronological history of the controversy over wetlands definitions.

   * Heimlich, Ralph E. and D. M. Gadsby. 1993. "Strategies for
     Wetlands Protection and Restoration."
     Cited above as entry 299.

390. Henderson, Rick. 1992. "The Swamp Thing." Pp. 791-798 in
     Rational Readings on Environmental Concerns, Jay H. Lehr, ed.,
     Van Nostrand Reinhold, New York, (reprinted from *Reason*
     April 1991).
     Presents several anecdotes regarding wetland delineation around the U.S.
     Concludes the current policies are not rational, but that rationality will
     return to wetlands policy once taxpayers are required to compensate
     landowners for wetlands.

391. Huffman, Robert Terry and Theda Braddock. 1992. *Waters of the
     United States: A Guide to Wetland Delineation, Jurisdiction, and
     Permits.* Lewis Publishing, Inc., Boca Raton, Florida, 800 pp.

392. Ibrahim, S. and I. Hashim. 1990. "Classification of Mangrove
     Forest by Using 1:40,000-Scale Aerial Photographs." *Forest
     Ecology and Management* 33/34(1/4):583-592.
     Study was done to identify the species groups of Peninsular Malaysian
     mangrove forest in aerial photographs, to delineate their distribution, and
     to quantify their coverage. Results show that there are three mangrove
     forest types that can be delineated with 90 percent correct interpretation.
     Concludes that mangrove forest can be delineated, classified, and mapped
     by using this scale of aerial photographs.

393. International Union for Conservation of Nature and Natural Re-
     sources (IUCN). 1990. *Directory of Wetlands of International
     Importance, Sites Designated for the List of Wetlands of Interna-
     tional Importance*, Montreax, Switzerland, 782 pp.

394. Johnston, Robyn M. and Michele M. Barson. 1993. "Remote
     Sensing of Australian Wetlands: An Evaluation of Landsat TM
     Data for Inventory and Classification." *Australian Journal of
     Marine and Freshwater Research* 44(2):235-252.
     This study aimed to develop simple remote-sensing techniques suitable for
     mapping and monitoring wetlands, using Landsat TM imagery of inland
     wetland sites in Victoria and New South Wales. It concluded that

satellite imagery is unlikely to replace aerial photography for detailed mapping of wetland vegetation types; however, satellite imagery has much to offer in monitoring changes in water regime and in reconnaissance mapping at regional scales.

395. **Josephson, J. 1992. "Status of Wetlands."** *Environmental Science Technology* **26(3):422.**
Presents a short summary of the U.S. Fish and Wildlife Service's 1991 report on the status and trends of U.S. wetlands and deepwater habitats in the contiguous 48 states. See entry 373.

396. **Kangas, P. C. 1990. "Energy Theory of Landscape for Classifying Wetlands." Pp. 15-23 in** *Ecosystems of the World 15: Forested Wetlands,* **David W. Goodall, ed., Elsevier Science Publishing Co., New York.**
Suggests wetlands can be classified using environmental energy sources. Applies the method to Georgia (U.S.) wetlands. Concludes that energy classification can contribute to better understanding than is now available from other appoaches. Included in entry 52.

* **Kantrud, Harold A., Gary L. Krapu, and George A. Swanson. 1989.** *Prairie Basin Wetlands of the Dakotas: A Community Profile.*
Cited above as entry 169.

* **Kent, Donald M. 1994.** *Applied Wetlands Science and Techonology.*
Cited above as entry 170.

397. **King, Wayne. 1992. "Slump vs. Wetlands in Trenton Bill to Revive Construction Permits."** *The New York Times,* **April 12, 141 (sec.1):47(l), col 1, 13 col.**
Discusses the implication of the passage of a New Jersey bill which automatically extends through 1994 all building permits which have expired in the last three years, thereby allowing development of areas previously held back because of wetlands regulations.

* **Kolawole, A. 1991. "Economics and Management of Fadama in Northern Nigeria."**
Cited above as entry 174.

398. **Kraus, Mark. 1993. "Wetland Identification and Delineation Manuals: Where are We?"** *Wetland Journal* **5(2):8,13.**
Discusses the shortcomings of the "three parameter approach" to wetland delineation and promotes the use of The Primary Indicators Method (PRIMET), which relies on a single parameter in most cases.

399. Kusler, Jon. 1992. "Wetland Delineation: An Issue of Science or Politics." *Environment* 34(2):6-11, 29-37.
The Bush Administration proposed a controversial new manual to define wetlands in 1991. Discusses definitions, the federal manual, and implications of alternative delineation policies. Concludes that the manual must be rewritten to define goals, separate policy from science, consider scientific evidence, and involve ultimate users.

* Kusler, Jon A. and Gail Brooks, eds. 1987. *Proceedings of the National Wetland Symposium: Wetland Hydrology.*
Cited above as entry 47.

400. Kuzila, M. S., D. C. Rundquist, and J. A. Green. 1991. "Methods for Estimating Wetland Loss: The Rainbasin Region of Nebraska, 1927-1981." *Journal of Soil and Water Conservation* 46(6):441-446.
Sought to estimate the areal extent of wetland lost between 1927 and 1981 in the Rainwater Basin of Nebraska. Used a 1927 soil survey as a baseline to compare to a 1981 survey and organized the data in a geographic information system framework (GIS). The greatest loss was 90 percent as determined within the GIS by comparing the 1927 soil survey and the 1981 National Wetlands Inventory data. The least loss was 35 percent as determined outside GIS by comparing the 1927 and 1981 soil surveys.

401. Laney, R. W. 1988. "The Elimination of Isolated and Limited-flow Wetlands in North Carolina." Pp. 243-254 in *Proceedings of the Symposium on Coastal Water Resources,* W. L. Lyke and T. J. Hovan, eds., Technical Publication, American Water Resources Association, Bethesda, Maryland.
An analysis of the loss of wetlands in two North Carolina counties which may possibly have environmental, economic, and legal ramifications.

402. Leary, Warren E. 1991. "In Wetlands Debate, Acres and Dollars Hinge on Definitions: Some Call New Rules a Victory for Reason--Others Fear Them." *The New York Times,* Oct. 15, 141:B8(N),C4(L), col 1.
Discusses the current controversy over the definition and delineation of wetlands. Outlines some of the regional issues in the debate, such as those concerning bottomland hardwoods, prairie potholes, and the Everglades.

403. Lehr, Jay H. 1992. "Wetlands: A Threatening Issue." Pp. 799-806 in *Rational Readings on Environmental Concerns,* Jay H. Lehr,

ed., Van Nostrand Reinhold, New York (reprinted from *Ground Water* 29(5):642-645).
Criticizes federal wetlands delineation procedures. Argues that vast amounts of groundwater are going unused because of wetland protection regulations. Claims that glorifying wetlands for purposes of political perceptions without explaining the risks and costs is unacceptable.

404. Lipske, Michael. 1991. "Floating in Controversy." *National Wildlife* 29(6):22-24.
Wetlands are an important part of farms, but Congress is considering a bill that would narrowly define *wetland*, thereby eliminating millions of acres of wetlands.

405. Lyon, John G. 1993. *Practical Handbook for Wetland Identification and Delineation*. Lewis Publishers, Boca Raton, Florida, 208 pp.
Presents characteristics and indicators of wetlands that are the focus of the federal jurisdictional wetland issue and strategies and methods for making wetland identification and delineation meet federal requirements.

406. Mader, Stephen F. 1991. "Wetland Boundaries and Classification." Pp. 705-710 in *TAPPI 1991 Environmental Conference (Book 2)*, San Antonio, Texas.

407. McGregor, Gregor I. 1992. "Wetlands Law Tests Government Power." *Environmental Protection* 3(9):42-49.
Wetlands and floodplain protection is one of the expanding and controversial fields of environmental control. This area is at the cutting edge of environmental protection because it is here that court cases are testing the outer limits of the police power and sovereign authority of federal, state, and local governments. Examples of local zoning and wetland bylaws illustrate the geographic variability. Working definitions of wetlands and floodplains do not necessarily mean the same thing in different statutes. It is important to review specific controls that apply to a project and to an area of the country.

408. McKee, P. M., T. R. Patterson, T. E. Dahl, V. Glooschenko, E. Jaworski, J. B. Pearce, C. N. Raphael, T. H. Williams, and E. T. LaRoe. 1992. "Great Lakes Aquatic Habitat Classification Based on Wetland Classification Systems." In *The Development of an Aquatic Habitat Classification System for Lakes*, W. Dieter N. Busch and Peter G. Sly, eds, CRC Press, Boca Raton, Florida.
Review and critique of three wetland classification techniques for the Great Lakes: (1) the Ontario Ministry of Natural Resources method

(score/point system), (2) the U.S. Fish and Wildlife Service method, and (3) geomorphic classifications. Included in entry 365.

409. **Megonigal, J. P., W. H. Patrick, Jr., and S. P. Faulkner. 1993. "Wetland Identification in Seasonally Flooded Forest Soils: Soil Morphology and Redox Dynamics."** *Soil Science Society of America* **57:140-149.**
Evaluates the use of hydromorphic soils to identify wetlands across the floodplain of the Savannah River, South Carolina.

410. **Moorhead, K. K. and A. E. Cook. 1992. "A Comparison of Hydric Soils, Wetlands, and Land Use in Coastal North Carolina."** *Wetlands* **12:99-105.**

411. **Morganweck, R. 1989. "Status and Trends of Wetlands in the Coterminous U.S."** *Renewable Resources Journal* **7(3):6-7.**

412. **Nilson, D. J. and R. S. Diamond. 1989. "Wetland Buffer Delineation Method for Coastal New Jersey."** Pp. 381-386 in *Wetlands and River Corridor Management: Proceedings of an International Symposium*, **Jon A. Kusler and Sally Daly, eds., Association of Wetland Managers, Inc., Omnipress, Madison, Wisconsin.**
Discusses the study designed to determine appropriate buffer widths to maintain the quality of water entering wetlands. Developed a reliable administrative tool, responsive to actual environmental conditions encountered in coastal New Jersey. Included in entry 177.

413. **Pearsell, William Grant. 1991.** *Wetland Boundary: Implications to Land Use Planning.* **M.A. thesis, University of Waterloo, Waterloo, Ontario, Canada, 155 pp., (University Microfilms Inc., Order No: AADMM-69124).**
Assesses wetland boundary determinations in southern Ontario for development purposes. Includes results of a survey of Ontario planners to determine delineation practices.

414. **Pettry, D. E. 1991. "Wetland Delineation."** Pp. 51-56 in *Proceedings of the 19th Annual Hardwood Symposium*, **paper presented at a "Symposium on Facing Uncertain Futures and Changing Rules in the 1990's," Starkville, Mississippi.**
Criticizes the *Federal Manual for Delineating Jurisdictional Wetlands* (entries 376 and 377) for not being subjected to scientific peer review or public hearings; having serious technical flaws; and being a lengthy, complex, and confusing document. Attacks the manual for its lack of objectivity essential for uniform application over the U.S.

415. Pierce, Robert J. 1990. "Testimony." *Status of the Nation's Wetlands and Laws Related Thereto,* Publication 101-69, Committee on Public Works and Transportation, Subcommittee on Water Resources, Washington, D.C.

416. Pierce, Robert J. 1990. "U.S. Wetlands Policy: A Modified Approach." *Water, Environment & Technology* 2(8):121, 122.
Criticizes the 1989 manual (entry 377). Suggests that non-wetlands may be as important or more important than some wetlands.

417. Pierce, Robert J. 1991. "Redefining Our Regulatory Goals." *National Wetlands Newsletter* 13(6):12-13.
Argues that "wetlands" has no ecological meaning; it is a social definition. Criticizes the 1989 manual (entry 377), especially the revised hydroperiod criterion. Suggests that a minimum period of inundation or saturation of 21 days be necessary before identifying something as wetland.

418. Pierce, Robert J. 1991. "Testimony." *Science of Wetland Definition and Delineation,* Publication 102, 102nd Congress, Committee on Science, Space and Technology, Subcommittee on Environment, Washington, D.C.
See entries 416 and 417.

419. Plaut, Josh. 1992. "What's a Wetland, Anyway?" *Science World* 48(13):2-6.
Briefly describes characteristics of wetlands and discusses their positive aspects on the surrounding environment.

420. Poiani, Karen A. and W. Carter Johnson. 1991. "Global Warming and Prairie Wetlands." *BioScience* 41:611-618.
Examines the potential consequences of global warming specifically for waterfowl habitat. Simulations indicate significant decline in habitat quality, from a nearly balanced cover water ratio to a nearly closed basin with no open water areas.

421. Pope, Kevin O., Eliska Rejmankova, Harry M. Savage, Juan I. Arrendondo-Jimenez, Mario H. Rodriguez, and Donald R. Roberts. 1994. "Remote Sensing of Tropical Wetlands for Malaria Control in Chiapas, Mexico." *Ecological Applications* 4:81-90.
Combines remote sensing, Geographic Information Systems (GIS), and field research to predict anopheline mosquito population dynamics in the Pacific Coastal Plain of Chiapas, Mexico.

422. **Prann, Ronald W. 1993. "Wetland Delineation Litigation: The Good, the Bad, the Ugly, A Case Study." Pp. 704-709 in** *Wetlands: Proceedings of the 13th Annual Conference of the Society of Wetland Scientists,* **Mary C. Landin, ed., South Central Chapter, Society of Wetland Scientists, Utica, Mississippi.**
Traces the history and conclusion of a lawsuit initiated by the property owner against the wetland consultant claiming improper delineation and loss of use of property. Included in entry 49.

423. **Ray, Dixy Lee with Lou Guzzo. 1993.** *Environmental Overkill: Whatever Happened to Common Sense?* **Regnery Gateway, Washington, D.C., 260 pp.**
Chapter 8, "Wetlands: The Land of the Free. . . ?", highlights some specific cases where individuals have had trouble with Section 404 and delineation issues. Discusses the 1987 and 1989 manuals. Concludes that the preservation and protection of all wetlands is a fine example of good intentions gone wild.

424. **Richards, William. 1994. "Wetlands: Let's Overproduce Them."** *AgriFinance* **(March):19.**
Concludes that the public and Congress have decided wetlands are important and are going to be protected. Offers several suggestions how agriculture can regain public trust while protecting property rights and values, such as the Wetland Reserve Program, wetland restoration, rental of wetlands for recreational uses, using wetland for water quality improvement, and selling wetlands to developers who need mitigation credits.

425. **Roman, C. T., R. A. Zampella, and A. Z. Jaworski. 1985. "Wetland Boundaries in the New Jersey Pinelands: Ecological Relationships and Delineation."** *Water Resources Bulletin* **21(6):1005-1012.**
Wetland protection regulations and guidelines often require the delineation of precise wetland boundaries on a case-by-case basis. In this study, conducted in the New Jersey Pinelands, an ecological characterization of vegetation composition, soil, and hydrologic relationships along upland to wetland *Pinus rigida*-dominated transitions provided the basis for a multiparameter approach to wetland boundary delineation. The transitional data set was analyzed by direct gradient analysis, cluster analysis, and ordination. It is concluded that vegetation composition can be a principal factor in delineating wetland boundaries along natural upland to wetland transitions. However, where distinct vegetation changes are not observed, a feature of our study sites, a multiparameter approach should be used.

426. **Roulet, Nigel. 1990. "Focus: Aspects of the Physical Geography of Wetlands."** *Canadian Geographer* **34:79-88.**
This 'Focus' article presents five examples of current research on the physical aspects of Canadian wetlands: (1) evaporation from wetlands, (2) the hydrological role of peat-covered wetlands, (3) hydrology and salinity of coastal salt marshes, (4) the biogeochemistry of small headwater wetlands, and (5) gas exchange between peatlands and the atmosphere. Concludes that a better understanding of the temporal and spatial variability of the physical, chemical, and biological processes of wetlands is required.

427. **Russell, James S. 1993. "Wetlands Dilemma."** *Architectural Record* **181:36-39.**
The use of wetlands has become an increasingly polarized issue, with environmentalists wanting to preserve natural areas and landowners wanting no use restrictions. Even the definition of a wetland is controversial. Details of wetland use and restrictions are explored.

428. **Schneider, Keith. 1991. "Proposal to Redefine 'Wetlands' Would End Curbs on Some Land."** *The New York Times,* **May 15, 140:A1(N) A18(L), col. 4.**
Discusses initial reaction to changes in the definition of federal wetlands regulations.

429. **Senjem, Norman. 1991. "Dueling Definitions: The War Over Wetlands."** *The Dakota Farmer* **109(12):8-10.**
Illustrates frustration of farmers over rapidly changing wetland delineation legislation.

430. **Sexton, Natalie R. 1994.** *Effects of Section 404 Permits on Wetlands in North Dakota.* **National Biological Survey Resource Publication 200, National Ecology Research Center, Fort Collins, Colorado, 16 pp.**
Reviews 87 wetland alterations from discharges of dredged or fill material in the Prairie Pothole Region of North Dakota. The discharges were authorized by nationwide permits (NWP) 13, 14, and 26 and by individual permits issued by the U.S. Army Corps of Engineers under Section 404 of the Clean Water Act during 1987-1991. Found that compliance by permit holders with special conditions was 85 percent. Ninety percent of the special conditions of individual permits were implemented by applicants. The effect on any one wetland from a discharge authorized by NWP 13 or NWP 14 seems to have been minimal; however, cumulative effects were not determined. The types and sizes of discharges authorized by NWP 26 were variable and did not seem to meet certain

regulatory requirements, for example, that they be similar in nature and have minimal individual and cumulative effects. Compliance by permit holders with permit conditions was greater than 75 percent. However, because some special conditions for individual permits pertained to implementation, compliance could not always be determined. More follow-up is needed of permitted discharges during and after implementation.

431. **Sinclair, Richard H., Jr., Mark R. Graves, and Jack K. Stoll. 1990. "Satellite Data and Geographic Information Systems Technology Applications to Wetlands Mapping."** *FWS Biological Report* **90(18):151-158.**

432. **Sipple, William S. 1992. "Time to Move on."** *National Wetlands Newsletter* **14(2):4-6.**
Develops a list of recommendations for consideration in developing wetland delineation manuals. Considers the 1989 federal manual (entry 377) the most technically sound delineation manual to date.

433. **Smigelski, Francis Thomas. 1992.** *Practical Use and Evaluation of the "Federal Manual for Identifying and Delineating Jurisdictional Wetlands" in New England.* **M.S. thesis, University of Massachusetts, Lowell, 147 pp., (University Microfilms Inc., Order No: AAD13-4789).**
The 1989 federal manual (entry 377) is evaluated in New England using 50 transects across a wetland boundary. Concludes that the status of hydrophytic vegetation on the National List for Region I were generally corroborated.

* **Steinhart, Peter. 1990. "No Net Loss: As Wetlands Vanish, We Begin to Recognize Their Value."**
Cited above as entry 231.

434. **Steinhart, Peter. 1993. "Mud Wrestling."** *Sierra* **78:54-63.**
A combination of water, plants, and soils define an area as a wetland. Developers and the petroleum industry have fought rules on wetlands protection, but the public is becoming more aware of their economic and ecological importance.

435. **Still, D. A. and S. F. Shih. 1991. "Using Landsat Data and Geographic Information System for Wetland Assessment in Water-Quality Management."** **Vol. 50:98-102 in** *Proceedings: Soil and Crop Science of Florida,* **Department of Agricultural Engineering, University of Florida, Gainesville.**

A Landsat Multispectral Scanner System analysis was used to classify spectrally unique wetlands areas within a river basin in Florida. Found that both the zoom transfer scope and the geographical information system (GIS) were very useful tools for wetland assessment from the Landsat data. Concludes that satellite data include the availability of new data for periodic updating of wetland information, and the potential of higher-resolution Thematic Mapper and SPOT imagery for achieving vegetation special identification and density analysis.

*   **Stockdale, Erik. 1992.** *Freshwater Wetlands, Urban Stormwater, and Nonpoint Pollution Control: A Literature Review and Annotated Bibliography.*
    Cited above as entry 232.

436. **SWCS. 1992. "SWCS Adopts Wetland Policy Statement."** *Journal of Soil and Water Conservation* **(Nov-Dec):439-440.**
    Briefly lays out SWCS wetland policy. With respect to definition and delineation, SWCS argues that (1) the definition should be scientifically valid and recognize regional variations, (2) the federal government should establish a procedure for administering agencies to develop regional guidelines and not legislate specific wetland delineation criteria, and (3) agencies at all levels of government must use equivalent definitions of wetlands for regulatory purposes.

437. **Teels, B. M. 1990. "Soil Conservation Service's Wetland Inventory." Pp. 93-103 in** *Federal Coastal Wetland Mapping Programs,* **Fish and Wildlife Service Biological Report 90(18), National Ocean Pollution Policy Board's Habitat Loss and Modification Working Group, Washington, D.C.**

438. *The Futurist.* **1993. "Wetlands versus Population Growth: As U.S. Population Grows, Wetlands Shrink." 27(5):55-56.**
    The U.S. Fish and Wildlife Service says that the continental U.S. has lost more than half of its original wetlands in a 200-year period, while increasing its population from 4 million in 1790 to 255 million in 1993.

439. **Tiner, Ralph W., Jr. 1989. "An Update of Federal Wetland Delineation Techniques." Pp. 13-23 in** *Wetlands: Concerns and Successes--Proceedings of a Symposium,* **David W. Fisk, ed., American Water Resources Association, Bethesda, Maryland.**
    Four key Federal regulatory and conservation agencies (Army Corps of Engineers, Environmental Protection Agency, Fish and Wildlife Service, and Soil Conservation Service) developed different approaches to identify wetlands to meet their own needs. In an effort to provide consistent

federal direction for identifying and delineating wetlands, the four agencies developed and adopted an interagency wetland delineation manual (the 1989 manual). Pertinent details of the 1989 manual are summarized. Included in entry 33.

440. **Tiner, Ralph W., Jr. 1990. "Use of High-Altitude Aerial Photography for Inventorying Forested Wetlands in the United States."** *Forest Ecology and Management* **33/34:593-604.**
The U.S. Fish and Wildlife Service selected high-altitude aerial photography as its primary data source for its inventory of U.S. wetlands through the National Wetlands Inventory (NWI). Stereoscopic interpretation of this photography is an efficient and cost-effective method for identifying, classifying, and inventorying wetlands on a national, regional, and statewide basis. Outlines procedures and summarizes experience in inventorying forested wetlands, emphasizing problems encountered and their resolution.

441. **Tiner, Ralph W., Jr. 1991. "How Wet is a Wetland?"** *Great Lakes Wetlands Newsletter* **2(3):1-4,7.**

442. **Tiner, R. W. 1991. "The Concept of a Hydrophyte for Wetland Identification."** *BioScience* **41(4):236-247.**
Gives examples of species occurring in wetlands and dry habitats. Examines the concept of hydrophyte as it relates to wetland identification and delineation. Argues that, in many cases, plant community composition is not conclusive in differentiating wetlands from non wetlands and other factors (i.e., landscape position, soil, and hydrology) must be considered.

443. **Tiner, Ralph W., Jr. 1991. "Wetland Delineation."** In *Proceedings of the 1991 Stormwater Management/Wetlands/Floodplain Symposium*, **G. Aron and E. L. White, eds., Department of Civil Engineering, The Pennsylvania State University, University Park.**

444. **Tiner, Ralph W. 1993. "The Primary Indication Method: A Practical Approach to Wetland Recognition and Delineation in the United States."** *Wetlands* **13:50-64.**
Discusses major limitations of current wetland delineation methods and offers an alternative method called the "primary indicators method." This new method is based on using features (national and regional plant and soil characteristics) unique to wetlands for identifying wetlands and their boundaries.

445. Toliver, John. 1993. "What are Wetlands? A Historical Overview." *Journal of Forestry* 91(5):12-14.
Provides an overview of the controversy over the criteria regulated for wetland definition and delineation. Discusses the parameters set forth in the 1987 (entry 376) and 1989 (entry 377) federal manuals as they relate to vegetation, soils, and hydrology. Discusses how the regulations apply to forested wetlands.

446. Turner, R. E. 1990. "Landscape Development and Coastal Wetland Losses in the Northern Gulf of Mexico." *American Zoologist* 30:89-105.
Investigates the extensive and increasing rate of wetland loss. Emphasizes causal agents with natural agents remaining constant and man-made influences accounting for much of the losses.

447. U.S. Congress. 1991. *The Impact of the Administration's Wetlands Proposals on Pennsylvania.* 102nd Congress, 1st Session, Oversight hearing before the Subcommittee on Energy and the Environment of the Committee on Interior and Insular Affairs, U.S. Government Printing Office, Washington, D.C., 154 pp.

448. U.S. Congress. 1991. *The Science of Wetland Definition and Delineation.* 102nd Congress, 1st Session, House Committee on Science, Space, and Technology, Subcommittee on Environment, U.S. Government Printing Office, Washington, D.C., 619 pp.

449. U.S. Department of Agriculture. 1990. *Secretary of Agriculture Yeutter Reports Wetland Losses Down During the 1980s.* Press Release, October 4, Office of Public Affairs, Washington, D.C.

450. U.S. Department of Interior. 1990. *Wetlands--Meeting the President's Challenge.* Fish and Wildlife Service, Washington, D.C., 31 pp.
The U.S. Fish and Wildlife Service's Wetlands Action Plan was prepared in response to the President's goal of no-net-loss of wetlands. The Action Plan draws on the Service's existing legislative authorities, regulations, and directives to focus and emphasize the Service's wetland conservation activities toward the goal of eliminating net loss of wetlands.

451. U.S. General Accounting Office. 1991. *Wetlands Overview: Federal and State Policies, Legislation, and Programs.* Fact Sheet for Congressional Requests, GAO/RCED-92-79FS, Washington, D.C., 93 pp.

Defines wetlands, discusses their importance, identifies quantity of wetlands, and provides an overview of federal and state wetlands-related policies, legislation, and programs.

452. **Vinzant, Larry and Joelle Buffa. 1988. "Considerations in Using the Multiple Parameter Approach to Delineate Wetlands in the San Francisco Bay Area."** Pp. **159-163** in *Proceedings of the National Wetland Symposium: Urban Wetlands,* **Jon A. Kusler, Sally Daly, and Gail Brooks, eds., Association of Wetland Managers, Inc., Berne, New York.**
Concludes that although the multiple parameter approach provides a consistent framework in wetland determinations, a complete spatial and temporal evaluation of the environmental setting must be made and all decisions tempered with professional judgements due to the uniqueness of the ecoregion. Included in entry 48.

453. **Walker, W. R. and S. C. Richardson. 1991.** *The Federal Wetlands Manual: Swamped by Controversy.* **Special Report No. 24, Virginia Water Resources Research Center, Blacksburg, 8 pp.**
Presents an overview of wetlands issues, stating the crux of the problem is that wetlands vary widely and some are not easy to define precisely. Identifies federal wetland agencies and state (Virginia) wetland agencies. Compares the 1989 (entry 377) manual and the 1991 proposed revisions.

454. *Wall Street Journal.* **1992. "Debate on Wetlands Apparently to be Left to Clinton to Resolve."** *Wall Street Journal,* **November 23, pA16(W) pA9(E).**
States that the Bush Administration has abandoned its efforts to redefine wetlands. Farmers argue areas are being protected that do not deserve protection. Also mentions the 1991 proposal to loosen the definition of a wetland.

455. **Want, William L. 1989. "Expanding Wetlands Jurisdiction Affects Property Transactions."** *The National Law Journal* **12(10):19.**

456. **Warner, William S. 1990. "A PC-Based Analytical Stereoplotter for Wetland Inventories: An Efficient and Economical Photogrammetric Instrument for Field Offices."** *Forest Ecology and Management* **33/34:571-581.**
Discusses the use of a personal computer (PC) based analytical plotter used by the USDA and several organizations in Norway. Found that its flexible application and cost make the system suitable for field office purposes. Examines other types of PC based equipment that can be used to make three dimensional images from aerial photographs.

457. Wilen, B. O. and R. W. Tiner. 1989. "National Wetlands Inventory-The First Ten Years." Pp. 1-12 in *Wetlands: Concerns and Successes--Proceedings of a Symposium*, David W. Fisk, ed., American Water Resources Association, Bethesda, Maryland. Included in entry 33.

458. Willard, Dan, Michele Leslie, and Robert B. Reed. 1990. "Defining and Delineating Wetlands." Pp. 111-136 in *Issues in Wetlands Protection: Background Papers Prepared for the National Wetlands Policy Forum*, Conservation Foundation, Washington, D.C.

459. Williams, D. C. and J. G. Lyon. 1991. "Use of a Geographic Information System Data Base to Measure and Evaluate Wetland Changes in the St. Marys River, Michigan." *Hydrobiologia* 219:83-95.
A digital data base was constructed by photo interpretation, mapping, and digitizing seven runs of aerial photography on the St. Marys River, Michigan. The database was used in conjunction with geographical information system software to examine historical changes in wetland area. There was greatest variation in areas of emergent wetland and scrub-shrub wetland, which appeared to be responding primarily to changes in water level.

460. Williamson, Lonnie. 1992. "What's a Wetland?" *Outdoor Life* 189(3):46-48.
The lack of a definition of a wetland in the 1972 Clean Water Act has led to disagreement over federal policy with regard to wetlands. Current discussions to define a wetland have raised controversy because the definition does not adequately protect the relative economic value of greenbelts and agricultural production.

461. Zentner, John. 1988. "Wetland Boundary Determinations in Urban Environments." Pp. 153-163 in *Proceedings of the National Wetland Symposium: Urban Wetlands*, Jon A. Kusler, Sally Daly, and Gail Brooks, eds., Association of Wetland Managers, Inc., Berne, New York.
Compares the results at three sites which a private firm delineated to the results of the same three sites using the U.S. Army Corps of Engineers and Environmental Protection Agency methods. Included in entry 48.

462. Zinn, Jeffrey A. and Claudia Copeland. 1993. *Wetlands Issues in the 103rd Congress*. CRS Issue Brief IB93025, Environment and Natural Resources Policy Division, Congressional Research Service, The Library of Congress, Washington, D.C., 11 pp.

A brief overview of wetland issues facing the 103rd Congress, including Section 404, mitigation and restoration, agriculture and wetlands, and funding for wetlands programs.

AUTHOR INDEX

GEOGRAPHIC INDEX

SUBJECT INDEX

About the Compilers

JAY A. LEITCH is Professor of Agricultural Economics at North Dakota State University. He has published widely and consulted internationally on wetland management. He has been a scientific advisor to the Assistant Secretary of the Army, a senior economist (IPA) in the Department of the Interior, and president of the Society of Wetland Scientists.

HERBERT R. LUDWIG, Jr., is a graduate research assistant in the Department of Agricultural Economics, North Dakota State University.

ISBN 0-313-29286-8

90000>

9 780313 292866

HARDCOVER BAR CODE